Jeremiah

A Study Guide for Congregations

Ernest D. Martin

Introduction by Millard C. Lind

HERALD PRESS
Scottdale, Pennsylvania
Kitchener, Ontario

JEREMIAH: A STUDY GUIDE FOR CONGREGATIONS
Copyright © 1978 by Herald Press, Scottdale, Pa. 15683
  Published simultaneously in Canada by Herald Press,
  Kitchener, Ont. N2G 4M5
International Standard Book Number: 0-8361-1878-2
Printed in the United States of America
Design: Alice B. Shetler

10 9 8 7 6 5 4 3 2 1

Contents

Introduction by Millard C. Lind — 3
Author's Preface — 7

1 Jeremiah: A Man and a Book (36, 45) — 9
2 Jeremiah's Call: Prophet to the Nations (1) — 16
3 Yahweh's Indictment and Call to Repentance (2:1—4:4) — 23
4 The Coming Judgment: How and Why (4:5—6:30) — 28
5 Jeremiah's Critique of Religion in Israel (7—10; 26) — 33
6 The Inner Turmoil of a Prophet (Selections from 11 to 20) — 38
7 Jeremiah's Message Dramatized and Symbolized (Selections from 13-27; 32; 35) — 43
8 Jeremiah's Oracles on Kingship (21—23:8) — 47
9 Jeremiah's Oracles on Prophets (23:9-40; 27—29) — 52
10 Prophecies to the Nations (25:15-38; 46—51) — 58
11 The Book of Consolation (30—33) — 64
12 Events Before and After the Fall of Jerusalem (34; 37—44; 52)—69
13 The Message of Jeremiah, Then and Now — 74

Introduction

Is biblical faith for easy times? Or is it for difficult times? I hope it is for both. But it is well to remember that in times of extreme crisis great men and women discovered that faith in God was the way to the future, not only for themselves but also for their people. When Israel was in slavery in Egypt, Moses discovered the way to liberation by faithful response to the God who met him at Sinai. When the Jews were subjugated by the Romans, Jesus dared to point to a new way from that of collaboration offered by the Sadducees, withdrawal by the Pharisees, or armed revolution by the Zealots. His daring cost Him His life.

The situation was no less difficult for Jeremiah. He proclaimed the collapse of the government, the end of the Judean state. Furthermore, he openly counseled the Jews to surrender to the enemy. This surrender, He insisted, was not merely one option among many for the Jews. God demanded it of them. To surrender was to choose life rather than death.

This message was not easy for Jeremiah. Jeremiah protested that his message resulted in his own isolation and suffering. The emphasis upon this tragic note is unique to Jeremiah among the prophetic books.

But Jeremiah's message was not only negative. He proclaimed that beyond God's judgment His thought for Israel would be salvation. Judgment for Israel would be but for 70 years, a crucible to purge the silver from the dross. That life beyond judgment would not be life as usual, but a new life inaugurated by a new act of God. That new act would deal with Israel's age-old problem—man's age-old problem. God would write His law, not upon tablets of stone, but upon the hearts of His people. Nowhere does the Old Testament come closer to the New than here.

Ernest Martin has written of these themes and more in this study guide to the Book of Jeremiah. The guide is of interest not only because of its challenging subject, but also because it was written by one who has dedicated his life to leadership in a congregation. One can hardly accuse Ernest of writing from an ivory tower. He is writing to the same kind of people to whom he ministers year after year.

There is something more of interest about this book. It was made possible by the people of Ernest's congregation. The book was born out of the inspiration of a year of study made possible for Ernest by his people. They saw the study of the Bible and theology not as "ivory tower" activity, but as something very much related to the life and work of the church. The book was born out of this partnership of ministry, congregation, and school.

I recommend this study book on Jeremiah to groups of believers everywhere. I recommend it because of its subject matter: how the Word of God in the words of Jeremiah shaped the life of the people of God in desperate times. I recommend it because of its author: a man who has devoted his life to serious study and teaching of this Word in the context of a congregation.

May the God who inspired Jeremiah inspire you who study His words, that through you we may receive a new word for our own chaotic times.

Millard C. Lind
Professor of Old Testament
Associated Mennonite Biblical Seminaries
Elkhart, Indiana

Author's Preface

Jeremiah is a rich book. But for many it is a closed book. Along with much of the Old Testament it is ignored as baffling, incomprehensible, and not relevant for us. This study guide arises out of a conviction that with a little help students of the Bible can not <u>only make sense out of Jeremiah</u>, but find it an exciting book.

What you have here is a study guide for a combination of individual and group study. Although not a commentary, it does contain explanations. You will also find a variety of exercises to stimulate discovery and help with study procedures. What you discover for yourself, even though it is not new, will mean more to you than what you are told it says. You will be encouraged to expose yourself to the text in a variety of ways, selected as seemed appropriate to the nature of the material being studied.

Of major concern is to <u>let the text speak for itself</u>, making primary use of material within the Book of Jeremiah. Not all persons will see the value of some of the exercises, especially in the first few lessons. But give it a try. The pieces will be seen to fit together as you get better acquainted with the book.

These lessons, although helpful for personal study, are intended for group study. They assume the value of sharing insights and gifts in study, and of testing conclusions by a group in which the Spirit is at work. The blanks are to be filled in in individual study. Then in the group opportunity should be given to compare answers, to raise questions, and to discuss items of interest. Questions without blanks provided are intended primarily for group consideration.

The group process needs leadership. The leader's job is to guide a process of study and sharing. A concise, readable commentary such as *The Layman's Bible Commentary*, Volume 12, by Howard Tillman Kuist, John Knox Press, 1960, can profitably be used by the leader (and all participants in the study) as a supplement to the lessons. Basically a self-help study guide, this course requires no additional leader's guide.

You should not be overly concerned immediately to make one-to-one applications to current issues. Rather than the air-route of hopping from isolated texts to present-day applications, the guide takes the ground-route of letting the text speak first in context. This method is sometimes more tedious, but also more reliable. Bridges to our experience will emerge, and can be worked at with integrity.

As mentioned earlier, Jeremiah is exciting but also difficult. The book contains a lot of material to cover, even in thirteen lessons. You will soon discover that the material in Jeremiah is not in chronolgical order. Nor is it entirely thematic or topical in arrangement. The writing and collecting process has left its imprint on the book. The approach of this series of lessons is topical, and that will sometimes mean skipping around in the book to bring similar passages together. Much of Jeremiah is in poetry form, which in itself makes it forbidding for many readers.

On the positive side, Jeremiah has a lot of narrative, with Jeremiah as the key person in the story. We have the privilege of learning to know the man through a variety of experience-centered information. You will find him a fascinating person.

The Revised Standard Version was used as the basic text in preparing the lessons. The name "Yahweh" has been used extensively, rather than the substituted title, "the LORD," found in many translations. Although it may not be a familiar name for many using this guide, it becomes comfortable with use and will grow on you if you give it a chance.

Expect to invest time in the study. There are no satisfactory substitutes. Some lessons can use more individual and group time than others. It will be an advantage not to be locked into a fixed time block for the group part.

In addition to *The Layman's Bible Commentary* volume mentioned above, several other resources may be found helpful. A good Bible dictionary will be useful. William L. Holladay's book, *Jeremiah: Spokesman Out of Time*, 1973, a Pilgrim Press book from United Church Press is stimulating and offers some alternative interpretations at points. Several chapters (12-14) of *God and His People* by Howard H. Charles, Herald Press, 1969, have concise background material on Jeremiah and his times. Several lessons call attention to some plays based on Jeremiah in *Judgment and Hope*, a book of plays by John W. Miller, Herald Press, 1972. These can be used to get in touch with the message and experiences of Jeremiah in a creative way. For persons interested in going into deeper study of Jeremiah, *The Anchor Bible* volume on Jeremiah by John Bright, Doubleday, 1965, needs to be considered.

The idea and inspiration for this study guide came while the author was enjoying the course on "Jeremiah" taught by Millard C. Lind at Associated Mennonite Biblical Seminaries in 1977. It seemed that exposure to the richness of Jeremiah should not be limited to the seminary classroom. Professor Lind's insights and emphases are no doubt reflected in these lessons, and his suggestions for sharpening up the manuscript were helpful. However, the author has developed the lessons out of his own study process and takes responsibility for the content and approach.

These lessons are provided to encourage and aid you to get acquainted with a prophet, a book, and a record of God's interaction with His people. The ultimate goal is that you may also know and interact with this same God whose fullest revelation is in the Lord Jesus Christ.

Ernest D. Martin

1. Jeremiah: A Man and a Book

Introduction

Focus. These studies in Jeremiah begin with a look at the prophet himself, his times, and the book that bears his name. Specifically, we will study (a) some of the biographical sections of the book and what they tell us about the man and his relation to his times; (b) the historical references that date these messages of Yahweh, noting the world events that led to crises in Israel; and (c) what the book says about how it came to be written. This session will provide background for the series of studies in Jeremiah.

Scripture. Scattered biographical accounts and time references; chapters 36; 45.

Prayer. Lord of all, with thanksgiving we look into a part of Your Word. You have spoken through the prophets, and we want to hear You and grow in our obedience. Thank you for the Holy Spirit to guide us and to teach us. We seek to honor You as we begin to get acquainted with Jeremiah. Amen.

What the Book Says About the Man

Jeremiah has more biographical material in it than any of the other books of the prophets in the Old Testament. Yet there is not enough information for a full-scale biography. For example, almost nothing about Jeremiah's early life or about the first fifteen years of his ministry is recorded. However, the few facts and isolated incidents scattered through the book provide an insight into the person of the prophet of God through whom the word of Yahweh came for more than forty years, spanning the reigns of the last five kings of Judah.

1. Biographical Data in the Book Itself

    a. Hometown: _____, 3 miles northeast of Jerusalem (1:1).

    b. Father: _____, who was a priest (1:1). Not the high priest of 2 Kings 22:4 ff but possibly a descendant of Abiathar (1 Kings 2:26 f).

    c. Call: In the _____ th year of _____, c. 627 BC (1:2).

    d. Associate and secretary (scribe): _____ (36:4-5).

  e. Marital status: _____ (16:1-4).
  f. List three incidents in Jeremiah's life you find in chapters 26—29; 34—39.

_____

_____

_____

  g. Popularity rating: _____ (20:1, 2; 26:11).

  h. Last days spent in _____ (43:4-7).

What initial impressions do you have of the man Jeremiah? What further information do you wish you had about this prophet as a man?

2. Jeremiah, a Prophet in Time

Jeremiah's personal life was intertwined with the history in which he lived. For example, not being permitted to marry, being imprisoned, and buying a piece of land were directly tied to the critical events of the times. He objected to his ministry, complained about his life, yet could not keep quiet. He kept on praying for the people even when God told him not to.

His message from Yahweh was closely tied to specific events and tides in the political and religious situation. Although spoken to specific situations, the prophet's message went beyond the times in which he lived.

What significance do you see in the observation that Jeremiah's personal life was directly affected by the events and pressures of the time in which he lived?

What the Book Says About the Times

1. Time Reference in Jeremiah

Jeremiah has a number of references to time that help to date the incidents. The next step in getting acquainted with the book is to get an overview of the history by pulling together the most significant dated material in the book. With the aid of the references on the left, fill in the data about years, rulers, and events in the blanks.

Reference	Dating concerning the kings of Judah	Dating concerning world rulers	Events
1:2, 3	13th year of Josiah		Jeremiah's call
25:1-3	_____	1st year of Nebuchadnezzar	
(_____ years from the 13th year of Josiah)			
32:1, 2	_____	_____	Siege of Jerusalem
36:1	_____		Writing of scroll

39:1	_____	_____
39:2	_____	_____
45:1	_____	_____
46:2	_____	Nebuchadnezzar defeated Neco at Carchemish
52:4	_____	_____
52:5, 6	_____	_____
52:12-14	_____ _____	Jerusalem burned

The Book of Jeremiah (is, is not) arranged in chronological order.

Compare these datings with 2 Kings 22—25 and 2 Chronicles 34—36.

Notice the cross-referencing of dates in 25:1-3; 32:1, 2, and 46:2. These enable a more precise dating.

Notice all that happened in the 4th year of Jehoiakim. Mark in color everything associated with that year.

2. *Summary of Events Leading Up to the Fall of Judah*

Study the list of persons and events below (with approximate dates) to get a sense of the chronology of the period. Mark the kings of Judah in the list. Check the dates against the information gleaned from your research in Jeremiah in the previous exercise.

722	Fall of Israel/Samaria to Assyria
687-42	Manasseh (pro-Assyrian policy)
645?	Birth of Jeremiah
642-40	Amon (pro-Assyrian policy)
639-09	Josiah (anti-Assyrian policy)
633	Beginning of steps of revolt against Assyria
627	Call of Jeremiah
622	Law book found (2 Kings 22:3 ff.)
612	Fall of Nineveh/Assyria
609	Death of Josiah (killed by Pharaoh Neco)
	Jehoahaz (Shallum, 3 months as king)
	Jehoiakim (Eliakim, set up as king by Pharaoh Neco)
605	Battle of Carchemish (Nebuchadnezzar defeated Neco)
598	Nebuchadnezzar came against Jerusalem, Jehoiakim's death
597	Jehoiachin (Coniah, 3 months as king)
	Zedekiah (Mattaniah made king, first deportation)
589	Zedekiah rebelled against Nebuchadnezzar (2 Kings 25:1)
587	Fall of Jerusalem, second deportation, Gedaliah governor of Judah
	Jeremiah to Egypt with remnant
582	Third deportation to Babylon (Jeremiah 52:28-30)

Use a Bible dictionary to find out the relationship of Josiah and the four kings that followed him.

3. Comment on the History

Jeremiah was the prophet of God in a most crucial time of Judah's history. Israel, the sister nation to the north, had been wiped out by Assyria nearly a century before. In the last quarter of the seventh century BC Judah was struggling for survival amidst the political tides of that part of the world. Judah was between Egypt and the eastern powers. When Assyria passed from the scene, Egypt stepped in. But Nebuchadnezzar of Babylon defeated Pharaoh Neco in 605. Babylon became the dominant power. The battle of Carchemish in 605 was a pivotal event and represented a major shift in power.

Israel had wanted, and gotten, a king like the other nations in order to cope with the Philistine crisis in the eleventh century. But nationhood and kingship proved to be a liability rather than an asset. The latter kings of Judah found themselves caught in the web of world politics. They engaged in political maneuverings, alliances, and revolts. Religious reforms got mixed in with political strategy, all making a very complex picture. Judah was a long way removed from the covenant relationship to Yahweh to which the people of God had been called.

God's prophets became the medium of God's leadership rather than the kings. Jeremiah pointed to another way in the confusion of the times. He spoke for Yahweh when Judah was headed for disaster. We will be discovering what Jeremiah's message was in further lessons.

4. Geography of the Middle East

The map shows the location of the major powers and the lesser nations around Judah in the time of Jeremiah. Because of the desert, travel from east to west was by way of the river valleys and coastal plains. As the armies of the empires marched back and forth from Egypt to Babylon they went through Palestine.

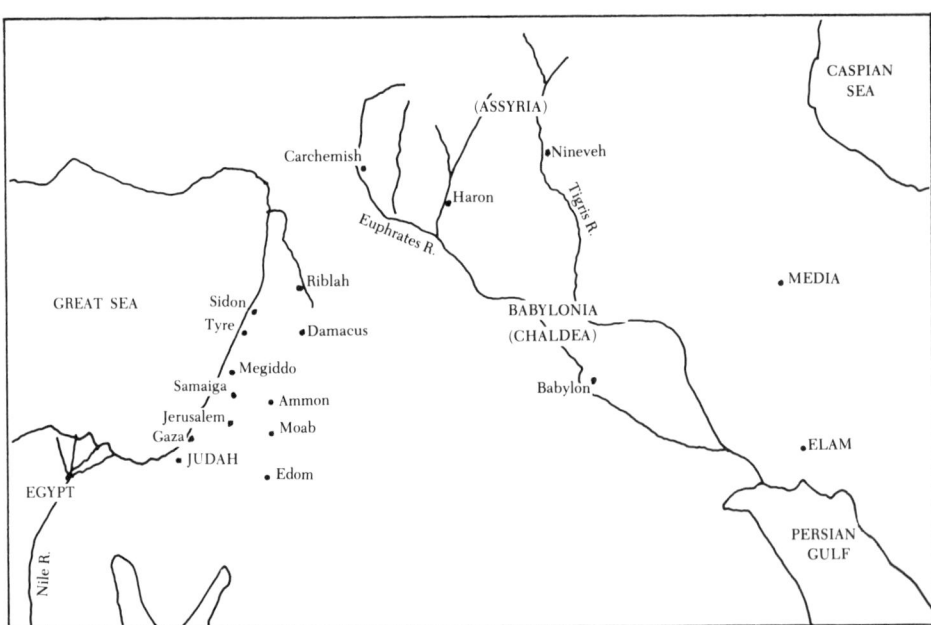

What the Book of Jeremiah Says about Itself

One feature of the Book of Jeremiah that is immediately apparent is that it is a mixture of prose and poetry, with about equal parts of each. Look at translations that set the poetry in poetic form, and note how these two basic types of literature are combined. Hebrew poetry is identifiable, not by rhyme, but by meter (which is not carried over in translations).

1. Types of Literature in Jeremiah

Several types of literature make up the book. Find at least one additional example of each of the types listed here, and record the reference(s). Some passages fit more than one category.

Autobiography (I, me): 1:9; _____

Biography (he, Jeremiah): 28:5 f.; _____
Oracle, pronouncement of Yahweh's word (usually poetry): 2:2b-3;

_____

Confession, the prophet's inner feelings and complaints: 12:1 f.;

_____

Prose historical narrative: 38; _____

Prose discourse: 31:31-34; _____

In further studies in Jeremiah you will want to be aware of and respect the type of literature you are reading.

2. Jeremiah 36 and the Writing of a Book

Chapter 36 provides unique insights into how a prophetic book such as Jeremiah came to be written. After reading the chapter, write in a title for each of the paragraphs indicated in the chart below, and answer the questions that follow.

Jeremiah 36

1-3	When did this take place? _____
4-7	Who commissioned the writing? _____
	What was the intended purpose? v. 3. _____

8-10	What was to be included?
11-19	How many years of ministry included? (25:3)
20-26	Method: dictation to _____ Writing materials and form: v. 18: on _____ with _____ v. 23: written in _____
27-32	What was different about the second scroll?

Chapter 45 also speaks of the writing of Jeremiah's words in a book, in the same year. Baruch's struggle with his involvement with Jeremiah and Yahweh's answer add a personal touch in our understanding of these servants of God. From what you know of the history of the times, what significance do you attach to the timing of this writing of the oracles Jeremiah had previously delivered?

3. *Observations on the Book's Development*
   a. The first step was the prophet's oral messages.
   b. The writing and collecting process began in 605 BC.
   c. The book goes beyond 605, with later additions made to the collection.
   d. There is virtually nothing biographical before 605.
   e. Jeremiah is not arranged in chronological order. (See 3:6; 21:1; 26:1; 32:1; 35:1).
   f. The organizing principle of the composite is at least partly thematic, and may also reflect the writing and collecting process.
   g. The Septuagint version (Greek translation of the Old Testament made before the time of Christ) has ⅛th less material than the Hebrew text and has chapters 46-51 immediately after 25:13, plus other differences. The Dead Sea Scrolls reveal that the Septuagint represents a different family of Hebrew manuscripts from the Massoretic text, commonly used for English translations. The fact that the New Testament frequently quotes from the Septuagint adds to its importance.
   h. As personal scribe to Jeremiah, Baruch seems to have had a prominent role in the writing. Much of the biographical material may be his work.
   i. Through Jeremiah, Baruch, and possibly other men of God, the Word

of Yahweh to His people was recorded, compiled, and preserved. What God said and did was faithfully written and continues as a part of the Scriptures—the Word of Yahweh to His covenant people.

j. The history of the book which is provided by the book itself in no way lessens its inspiration or its importance, but enriches our appreciation for Jeremiah and the Bible as a whole.

What insights or questions do you now have concerning how a prophetic book, and Jeremiah in particular, came to be written?

4. Major Components of the Book of Jeremiah

No fully consistent outline can be imposed on Jeremiah. However, three fairly clearly defined sections can be identified: (a) The Book of Doom, 1:1—25:13. (b) The Book of Consolation, 31—33. (c) The Book of Prophecy to the Nations, 46—51. Chapters 26—30 and 34—45 are largely biographical narrative. Chapter 52 is an historical appendix.

For Review and Summary

If you need to, check back into the lesson materials for the answers.

1. List three important events, with dates, that are an integral part of the historical setting of Jeremiah.

    a. _____

    b. _____

    c. _____

2. Recall what you consider the major facts of Jeremiah's life and circle one or two that were directly intertwined with his ministry and message.

_____

_____

3. Record three things about how Jeremiah came to be written that you want to remember.

    a. _____

    b. _____

    c. _____

Jeremiah's life and ministry were deeply affected by the times in which he lived. He was a prophet in time. Yet his message was from Yahweh. He heard a different drumbeat from what his peers were following. How can we be in dialogue with our culture and yet not be squeezed into its mold?

2. Jeremiah's Call: Prophet to the Nations

Introduction

Focus. Jeremiah's right to speak for Yahweh rested on his call. Chapter 1 includes an account of the prophet's call. In this lesson we will learn (a) the features of Jeremiah's call, (b) how it compares with other call accounts in the Bible, (c) the role and authority of the prophet in Israel, and (d) the emphasis on "the word of Yahweh" in Jeremiah.

Scripture. Primarily Jeremiah 1.

Prayer. God of grace and God of wisdom, we acknowledge You as the God of Your people. Thank you for stepping into the human scene and touching lives. Again it is our privilege and responsibility to search the Scriptures. We want to open our eyes and ears to Your word and to You. We want to know how You called Jeremiah so that we can know and follow Your call to us in Jesus. Quicken us by Your Spirit for Your name's sake. Amen.

Study of Jeremiah 1

1. The Text

First we engage in direct Bible study in the chapter and then explore some of the themes that emerge. The text of Jeremiah 1 printed below is the translation of John Bright in *The Anchor Bible*. It is printed here with room for some notes in the margin to make careful study of the chapter easier.

Jeremiah 1

1 The sayings of Jeremiah ben Hilkiah, of the priestly family that lived in Anathoth in the land of Benjamin, 2 to whom the word of Yahweh came in the days of Josiah ben Amon, king of Judah, in the thirteenth year of his reign 3—and also in the days of Jehoiakim ben Josiah, king of Judah, and down to the end of the eleventh year of Zedekiah ben Josiah, king of Judah, that is, to the deportation of Jerusalem's population in the fifth month of that year.

4 The word of Yahweh came to me, thus:
5 "Before I had formed you in the womb I chose you;
   Before you were born I set you apart,

>   And appointed you prophet to the nations."
> 6 Then I said, "Ah, my Lord Yahweh! I don't know how
>   to speak. I'm only a boy!"
> 7 But Yahweh answered,
>   "Never say, 'I am only a boy';
>   For you'll go on what errands I send you,
>   And you'll say what I tell you to say.
> 8 Don't be afraid of them!
>   For I'm with you to come to your rescue—
>   Yahweh's word."
> 9 Then Yahweh stretched out his hand and touched my mouth.
>   And Yahweh said to me:
>   "There! I have put my words in your mouth.
> 10 See! I have made you an overseer this day
>   Over nations and kingdoms,
>   To uproot and tear down,
>   To destroy and to raze,
>   To build and to plant."

11 And the word of Yahweh came to me thus: "What do you see Jeremiah?" I said, "An almond rod is what I see." 12 Then Yahweh answered, "You see very well! For I am watching over my word to perform it."

13 The word of Yahweh came to me a second time: "What do you see?" And I said, "What I see is a bubbling pot, and it is tipped from the north." 14 Then Yahweh said to me:

> "From the north will disaster be loosed
>   Upon all who dwell in the land.
> 15 For see! I am calling
>   All the kings of the north—Yahweh's word—
>   And they will come and will each set his throne
>   Right in front of Jerusalem's gates,
>   Against all her surrounding walls,
>   Against each of Judah's towns.
> 16 So I'll utter my sentence upon them
>   For their tale of wrong in forsaking me,
>   In sending up offerings to other gods,
>   And bowing down to their own handiwork.
>
> 17 As for you—gird up your loins!
>   Stand up and say to them
>   Whatever I tell you to say.
>   Don't lose your nerve because of them,
>   Lest I shatter your nerve right before them.

18 And I—see! I have made you today
   A fortified city,
      An iron pillar,
   A wall of bronze
      Against all the land:
   Against Judah's kings and princes,
      Its priests and landed gentry.
19 Attack you they will; overcome you they can't,
   For I'm with you to come to your rescue—
                                    Yahweh's word."

2. Observations on the Text

a. Literary features. Note that there are prose and poetry, biography and autobiography, oracles (here as God's Word to Jeremiah), and dialogue (He said... I said...).

b. Divisions. Test the divisions indicated in the text: 1-3, 4-10, 11-12, 13-16, 17-19. Write appropriate titles for the sections in the margin.

c. Some things to mark in the text. Several colors of pencils or highlighters will make the repeated words and phrases stand out:
   "the word of Yahweh" (4x) "my words" (1x)
   "Yahweh's word" (3x)
   the 4 verbs in v. 5 (formed, chose, etc.)
   the 6 infinitives in verse 10b (to uproot, to tear down, etc.)
   "what(ever) I tell you to say" (2x)
   "I'm with you to come to your rescue" (2x)
   "nations" (2x)

3. Notes on the Text

Verse 3. The heading (vv. 1-3) covers most of what is included in the book, but not all. Chapters 40—44 and the last part of 52 come after the fall of Jerusalem.

Verse 5. "Formed" is a potter's word (Genesis 2:7, 19; Psalm 139:13). "Chose" means knew or foreknew, therefore implying a special relationship (Amos 3:2). "Set apart" means consecrated for special use (Exodus 28:41). "Appointed" is gave in Hebrew, meaning to set in place (Genesis 41:41). Since birth determined nationality, consecration before birth is significant for one designated as "prophet to the nations."

Verse 6. Jeremiah could talk back to Yahweh. The call had freedom built into it, even though Jeremiah later complained of being overpowered. "Boy" has the meaning of youth, unmarried, without social or political status. Jeremiah said he could not speak among the elders because he was not yet an elder. Yahweh set him straight about that.

Verse 9. The word Jeremiah spoke was not Jeremiah's, it was placed in his mouth. His message was not the product of philosophical musings.

Verse 10. Jeremiah's assignment included negative and positive elements.

Verses 11-12. There is an untranslatable wordplay in these verses. The word "almond" has only one vowel different from the word "watching."

Verse 13. "A second time" makes the first time the vision in verse 11. The two visions stand alongside the description of call in verses 4-10.

Verse 15. The reference to what is coming from the north is expanded in chapters 4—6.

Verse 16. "Them" refers to all who dwell in the land (of Judah), verse 14.

Verses 17-19. This last section is closely related to verses 4-10. It is a summary of the personal charge and promise of Yahweh to Jeremiah. God's "witness" does not exclude hardship and suffering.

4. Comparisons

a. Compare Jeremiah's title phrase with that of other books of prophets. Write in the corresponding phrases.

Jeremiah 1:1 The words of Jeremiah . . . to whom the word of Yahweh came.

Hosea 1:1 _____

Amos 1:1 _____

Micah 1:1 _____

Zephaniah 1:1 _____

Malachi 1:1 _____

What similarities and differences do you observe?

b. Call narratives. The call narratives in the Bible have an observable pattern to them, with variations. Indicate which verses (or parts of verses) fit with each of the elements in Jeremiah's call. For the calls of Moses and Gideon see if the elements are found in the passages and put a check mark in the blank for each element you find.

Pattern of Call	Jeremiah 1:4-10	Moses Exodus 3:1—4:17	Gideon Judges 6:11-24
Confrontation	_____	_____	_____
Introductory word	_____	_____	_____
Commission	_____	_____	_____
Objection	_____	_____	_____
Reassurance	_____	_____	_____
Sign	_____	_____	_____

What other accounts of God's call to persons in the Bible can you recall?

c. Consecration before birth. Compare Jeremiah 1:5 with Isaiah 49:5, 6 and Galatians 1:13-16. What similarities do you see? Who corresponds to Jeremiah in these two accounts? What do you make of this comparison?

Themes in Jeremiah 1

1. The Prophet Jeremiah's Authority

A number of factors contribute to Jeremiah's convincing awareness of call. Yahweh came to him in a multimedia communication:

a. Jeremiah heard. Which verses say what he heard? _____

b. Jeremiah felt. What did he feel? _____

c. Jeremiah saw. What did he see? _____

Additional elements add to the certainty of Jeremiah's authority as a prophet: his objection was answered, he was sent (v. 7), he was reassured that God watched over his word (v. 12), he was promised power (v. 18), and he was promised God's presence (vv. 8 and 19).

Read Jeremiah 23:16-22. Where does the true prophet get his message according to verses 16 and 22? Although not included in chapter 1, from this later passage it becomes clear that Jeremiah knew he got his message in the heavenly council and reported what he heard there.

The prophet's authorization became an issue repeatedly. Jeremiah was challenged by kings, princes, priests, and prophets. He had his own inner struggles. Yet he did not keep quiet.

2. The Prophet Jeremiah's Role

The designation "prophet to the nations" begs for special attention. Notice that Jeremiah was not appointed prophet to Israel and Judah *and* the nations, but simply prophet to the nations. Yet in practice Jeremiah's message was directed primarily to Judah. The oracles to the nations in 46—51 are in the book of the people of God. Whether the nations ever got those messages is not reported.

So what does this mean that Jeremiah was a prophet to the nations? He did not have two ministries, one to Judah and one to the nations. God spoke to the nations through His people. Jeremiah was in fact speaking to the nations as he brought Yahweh's message to Judah. What Jeremiah was to Israel and Judah, Israel and Judah were to the nations, and Christians are to be to the world. God's sovereignty includes the whole world, but He works through His people, and through His prophets.

From Jeremiah 1 it becomes clear that Jeremiah was commissioned as God's chief representative. He was given a monumental, lonely task. Although kings, prophets, and priests continued up to Judah's end, the faithful prophet became the principal channel of Yahweh's communication with His people. Human kings had usurped Yahweh's place as king of His people.

Further, kings (as well as prophets and priests) were to function with the law (Torah) as their power base. See Deuteronomy 17:18-20. The heart of Yahweh's expressed will (Torah) was His revelation in word and act through Moses. Torah was to be the base for power, wisdom, word, and action. The intended arrangement may be visualized like this.

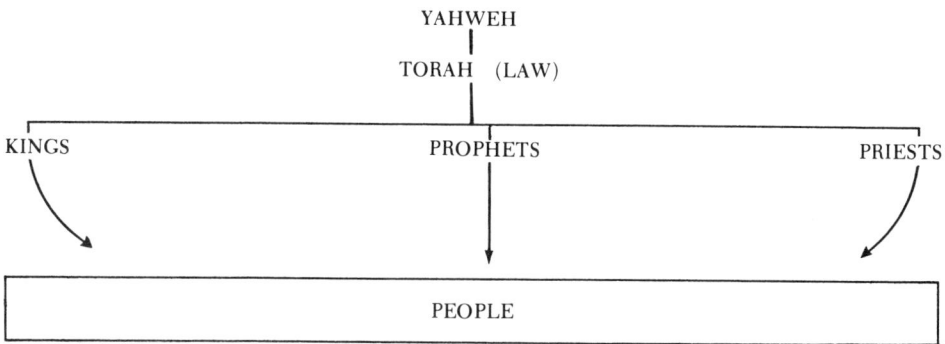

But the kings rejected Torah as their base and took the power base of military, political, and economic power. The priests and people also accepted the power base of the surrounding nations. The message of most of the prophets in Jeremiah's time was not based on Torah, as will come out in a later lesson. Thus Jeremiah found himself in tension with kings, princes, prophets, priests, and people.

In chapter 36, which we studied in the first lesson, you will recall that Baruch first read the scroll to the people and later it was read to the king. No doubt part of what angered the king was that Jeremiah had bypassed him and gone directly to the people.

The church faces similar issues today. Discuss the temptations to reject the teachings and Spirit of Jesus and to rely on financial, military, and political power and human wisdom.

3. *"The Word of Yahweh"*

This phrase occurs more than 50 times in Jeremiah plus many more instances of "word" or "words" in which the meaning is "the word of Yahweh." The term "word" has a broader meaning than the common English usage, where it means verbal symbol. Sometimes the Hebrew word is translated "thing." In Hebrew thought, word and event are not separated as we usually separate them. What God says, He does. His word is fulfilled in the event. (See Isaiah 55:10, 11.)

A related phrase, "Yahweh's word" (or "says the Lord") punctuates Jeremiah some 170 times. It stands as an identifying mark of the oracles of Yahweh. Its meaning is utterance or oracle of Yahweh. You have noted and marked both of these expressions in chapter 1. Now look through chapters 2—6, watching for additional occurences. Compare translations for other ways these phrases have been rendered into English.

Why do you think these expressions occur so often in Jeremiah? What impression do you get as you see them repeated?

It is too early in the study of Jeremiah to make a full statement about what is included in the "word" that came through Jeremiah. But we already have hints in chapter 1. Verses 10, 14-16 speak of judgment. Verse 10 also has the note of hope. An indictment of sins is mentioned in verse 16. The critique of religion in Judah in later chapters will explain more of how God's people were forsaking their covenant relationship with Yahweh.

Review and Reflection

1. List five things about Jeremiah's call that you want to remember.

   a. _____

   b. _____

   c. _____

   d. _____

   e. _____

2. List three of the ways Jeremiah could know he was an authorized spokesman for God.

   a. _____

   b. _____

   c. _____

3. Jeremiah's call was tailored to a specific person at a specific time. In what ways is the call of God different or similar today? What authorization does the church have? What authorization do you have?

4. Jeremiah's "weapon" was Yahweh's word, rather than the political and military weaponry used by the nations, including Judah. Is this not the same power base for God's representatives today? What does it mean for Christians to be armed with the word of Yahweh in a world gone mad with economic power and military armaments?

5. What does it mean to live by all that proceeds from the mouth of God? The profoundness of "the word of Yahweh" is missed when it is simply equated with the Bible. "The word of Yahweh" is a lot more than the magic of Bible words and verses. The whole of God's revelation is His word, including the Word become flesh. What needs to happen for the word of Yahweh to pervade our lives and message as it did Jeremiah's?

3. Yahweh's Indictment and Call to Repentance

Introduction
Focus. What was Jeremiah's message which Yahweh put in his mouth? For answers we will explore the first examples of his oracles in the early chapters of the book. In chapter two dealing with God's indictment of His People we will note the description of Israel's and Judah's sins and the charges brought against them. We will look into the meaning of repentance according to Jeremiah, what it is and what it is not. How the message of repentance related to Josiah's reforms will be of particular interest.
Scripture. 2 Chronicles 34; Jeremiah 2:1—4:4.
Prayer. Thank you, Lord, for redeeming us from the ways of rebellion and worthlessness. You know us as we are. You love us in our perversity and pretense. How great You are. Help us as we look at the issue of our loyalty to You and the honesty of our repentance. Without Your Spirit's voice we so easily delude ourselves. Speak to us through Jeremiah. We commit ourselves to hear, for Jesus' sake. Amen.

Historical Setting
In 722 BC the northern kingdom, Israel, experienced God's judgment at the hands of the Assyrians. However, not all the people were deported. From time to time the southern kingdom, Judah, expressed interest in the northern tribes. The prophets as well as the kings were interested in those people. Jeremiah spoke of Israel as well as of Judah. Sometimes he referred to the whole of God's people as Israel. Watch carefully for the intended meaning of such terms as Israel, Jacob, Judah, and Jerusalem. The designation Israel is used in both the broad sense (the Old Testament people of God) and the narrow sense (the northern kingdom) in these lessons.

Very early in his reign Josiah initiated some reform measures. They appeared as religious reforms although they were politically motivated in part. One way of disassociating a nation from the domination of another nation is to get rid of the other nations gods. Read 2 Chronicles 34 for a review of those reform measures, especially verses 1-4, 8, 14, and 29-33. Note that some steps were taken before the lawbook was found in 622. Jeremiah did not specifically refer to Josiah's reforms, but part of what he said about repentance seems to fit those times. According to Jeremiah 22:15, the prophet held king Josiah in high regard. Yet there is a lot of evidence scattered through his oracles that stands as a sharp critique of the reform movement because of its methods and shallowness.

What changes did Josiah make?

_____

How did he make the changes?

_____

Jeremiah was in that uncomfortable situation of criticizing an effort that had some good points about it and which seemed on the surface to be moving in the right direction. In what ways can you identify with that kind of "yes, but" tension?

The Sin and Unfaithfulness of Yahweh's People (Chapter 2)
1. A Chapter in Three Parts
    a. Verses 1-3 tell of the "honeymoon days" which stand in contrast to the days of the prophet.

    b. Verses 4-13 are in lawsuit form, in which Yahweh brings his case against His people. This section has a close resemblance to several other Old Testament passages. Before getting into the specifics of God's charges against His people in Jeremiah 2, read one or more of the following passages to get acquainted with this form of God bringing an indictment against the people of the covenant: Deuteronomy 32:1-25; Psalm 50, Isaiah 1:2-20; Micah 6:1-8.

These are examples of a covenant lawsuit. The word "contend" in Jeremiah 2:9 is a legal term. As you study the lawsuit in Jeremiah 2:4-13 note the features:

Who are the witnesses (v. 12)? _____

Who are the defendants (vv. 4,9)? _____

What is the basis of appeal (vv. 6-7)? _____

How is the charge expressed (v. 11)? _____

    c. Verses 14-37 are made up of various oracles on the same theme, Yahweh's indictment of the people's unfaithfulness to covenant.

2. Figures Used in the Chapter
Write in the figure found in each of the following verses. (For example, in verse 2 marriage and in verse 13 cisterns.) Do you understand the meaning in each case?

v. 2 _____

v. 13 _____

v. 14 _____

v. 18 _____

v. 20 _____

v. 21 _____

v. 22 _____

v. 23 _____

v. 24 _____

v. 32 _____

3. *Charges Yahweh Leveled Against His People*
Comb through the chapter and list the charges with references. (The findings of others in the study group may supplement your list.)

a. _____

b. _____

c. _____

d. _____

e. _____

f. _____

g. _____

What one word seems to you to best express the nature of Israel's sin?

_____

4. *Notes and Questions*
Baal worship had a lot of appeal to agricultural people because of the emphasis on fertility. Fertility means increased property. Baal worship was seen as a shortcut to wealth. The worship was also grossly sensual. Sacred prostitution was a regular feature. The references in Jeremiah 2 to harlotry and sexual lust apply in part to the sexual perverseness and looseness of Baalism. But serious as that was, the even greater sin which is labeled harlotry was the unfaithfulness to Yahweh expressed by the passionate interest of God's people in running after other gods.

The last line of 2:5 is vivid. Chasing after worthlessness they became worthless. Chasing after gods that are nothing, the people became nothing. The historical reference is to the northern kingdom and its tragic end in 722 BC. Several other times in the chapter reference is made to things that "do not profit." What searching after things that are empty is going on today, and how does it leave people empty?

In 2:5 God speaks as a hurt lover, asking in effect, "What's wrong? What did I do to deserve this from you?" What aspects of God's character stand out in this questioning?

Yahweh's Call to Repentance (3:1—4:4)

After the indictment of sins in chapter 2 we hear the voice of God calling His people to repentance in chapter 3. The word "return" (or "turn") occurs 8 times in 3:1—4:4. Other forms of the Hebrew word for return and turn are found an additional 6 times in the passage. For example, in 3:22 the piling up of words is something like: "Return, turnable sons, and I will heal your turnings" (Holladay). The term includes turning from and turning to. Mark all of these related words in your study Bible.

From what you see in this passage, what is the meaning of the repentance God calls for? What is God's attitude? Is it easier to turn away from God than to turn back to Him? Why? Share your findings and understandings.

Note the references to shallowness in repentance. How is it expressed?

3:5 _____

3.10 _____

Relate this to Josiah's reforms. Why were they bound to fail? Read Romans 2:28, 29 with Jeremiah 4:4. What does circumcision of the heart add to the meaning of repentance?

3:21—4:2 is a liturgical dialogue that illustrates the danger of hollow words without real change. Decide in the study group which part was spoken by the prophet, which by Yahweh, and which by the people. Assign the roles, then read it. Does this sound like anything you have done in church?

Repentance is viewed in Jeremiah as the covenant renewal of a people. Repentance is individual, but it is more than individual. Evaluate this statement: "Repentance is not a slight, gradual mid-course correction toward greater personal integrity which takes place purely individually, but is a fundamental transfer to a new kingdom, a whole turning to Yahweh in the context of a covenant community."

What one word best describes repentance for you?

Review and Summary

1. List five of the charges Yahweh brought against His people through Jeremiah. See Chapter 2.

a. _____

b. _____

c. _____

d. _____

e. _____

2. State two weaknesses in Josiah's reforms as evaluated by the meaning of true repentance.

a. _____

b. _____

3. What criteria can be used to test the genuineness of repentance? Refine your conclusions in the group process.

_____

_____

_____

"Born again" is a status openly claimed by many prominent people in entertainment, sports, and politics. Assess the level of repentance and change involved when the lifestyle and life interest of "born again" persons still includes commercialism, extravagance, violence, the glory of stardom, being the idols of millions, and being an integral part of industries that are counter to the kingdom of Christ. Compare Jeremiah's emphasis with John the Baptist's words, "Bear fruit that befits repentance" (Mt. 3:8)

4. A lot of questions are asked in 3:1—4:4. What is one question that caught your attention? What meaning does it have for you?

_____

_____

_____

_____

For supplemental study, read articles on repentance in Bible dictionaries.

4. The Coming Judgment: How and Why

Introduction
Focus. This lesson gives an exposure to a block of oracles on a common theme. Without dates, it is not certain when they were written, but they give a good sampling of prophecies of judgment. Of particular interest are (a) descriptions of coming judgment from the north, (b) reasons for that pending judgment, and (c) the interaction between the prophet Jeremiah and Yahweh. These passages must be seen in the seventh century BC setting before attempting to determine their relevance for today.

Scripture. Jeremiah 4:5—6:30.

Prayer. God of truth and love, You have been struggling through the centuries with Your people. What was written about the experiences of Your people in the Old Testament we accept as examples and warnings. Sharpen our spiritual perception by Your Spirit as we search out Your message in a part of Jeremiah. Reveal Yourself to us in the Word and enable us to see ourselves in Your mirror. For this we thank and praise You in the name of Jesus. Amen.

Nature of the Material

What are the handles on a section of Scripture such as we have in this lesson? The concepts, themes, and message are not obvious after the first reading. Let's take stock of what we have here. Most translations indicate a mix of prose and poetry, although there isn't agreement on how much is poetry. The section has some earmarks of being a collection of oracles, (pronouncements of Yahweh's word), yet a pattern of organization stands out. A repeated theme is the enemy from the north. Descriptions of destruction coming from the north are followed by reasons for judgment and responses from the people, the prophet, and Yahweh.

Notice the pattern of movement from north to south, from Dan (4:15) to Tekoa (6:1). At first the move is to be to the cities for safety and later when the doom of Jerusalem is evident the move is to be away from the cities to the hills (4:5; 6:1).

A standing question for the reader is, who is speaking, and to whom? At points Yahweh is identified as the Speaker, but He is not the only one speaking. One feature of chapter 5 is a number of questions. In each case state the essence of the question in your own words, who is asking the question, and of whom? (The references indicate the questions as found in RSV.)

	Question	By whom	To whom
Verse 3	_____	_____	_____
Verse 7	_____	_____	_____
Verse 9	_____		
	_____	_____	_____
Verse 19	_____	_____	_____
Verse 22	_____	_____	_____
Verse 29	_____		
	_____	_____	_____
Verse 31	_____	_____	_____

Outline

The following outline, suggested in *The Layman's Bible Commentary*, attempts to convey the organization of the section. Note the shift back and forth between description-prediction and reason-response. A few exceptions to the outline can be found. Test it in your own reading and study.

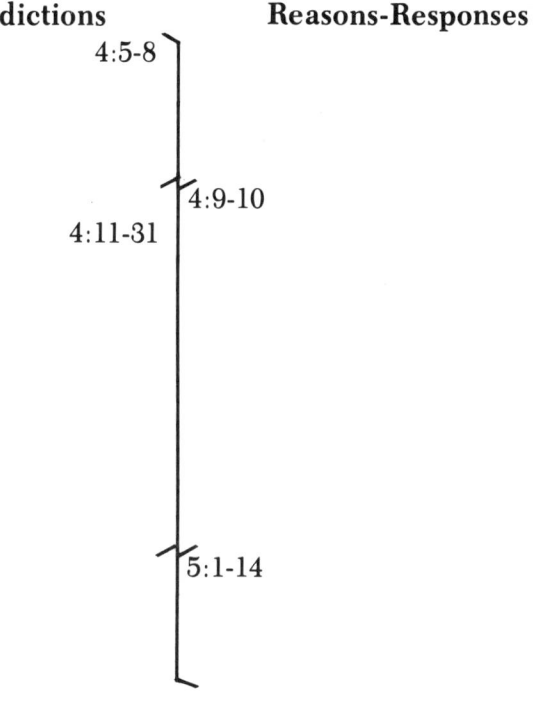

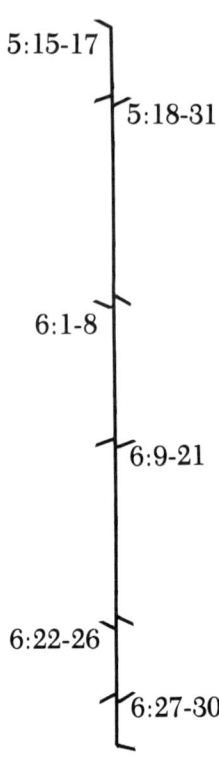

Use the space above to record key words and ideas as you work through the material yourself. Note what you find of interest and importance in each of the alternating divisions.

Themes

1. Description of What Is Coming from the North

The modern equivalent of the first part of 4:5 would be, "Sound the air raid alarms!" The announced threat is imminent disaster and destruction coming from the north. It was an external threat.

Note the many descriptive words in the sections telling of the enemy from the north. The enemy is like a "lion" and other wild animals. He is like the scorching "wind" and like "clouds." See 4:23-28. It reads like a reversal of the creation account according to Genesis 1, in which all goes back to waste and void. The noise of the approaching enemy is mentioned. The fierceness of the attackers and of the attack stands out.

What invading army is being described as descending on Judah and Jerusalem? Two possibilities have been proposed. One is the Scythian hordes originating in the Black Sea area. But some elements of regimented army attack do not fit the style of the Scythians. The other is the Chaldeans (Babylonians). Although Babylon was to the east, rather than the north, traffic moved by way of the river valleys so that the Babylonian armies would in fact come from the north. (Review the geography by referring to the map in Lesson 1.)

Exactly who that external enemy would be is not of major importance. Of greater significance is who is behind the invasion and destruction. There is no question who is behind the action. See 4:6, 8; 5:15 for direct statements regarding the source. The idea of God making war on His people is shocking. The one who defended His people, even led them in holy war, is about to pour out judgment on Israel.

Reread aloud in the study group the sections describing the coming invasion and destruction (the passages on the left side of the outline above.) Imagine the sights and sounds so vividly described. How do such predictions make you feel?

2. Reasons for Judgment

There are plenty of answers to why, scattered through the oracles. Most of them show up in the passages on the right of the outline. Make a list of the specific sins which justified Yahweh's action against His people. Begin with 5:1. Can you find 10 reasons?

_____   _____

_____   _____

_____   _____

_____   _____

_____   _____

Verse 20 in chapter 6 anticipates what we will take up in the next lesson. The last section of chapter 6 rests on the refining figure. Verse 30 has a play on words that can be expressed by: "Refuse silver they are called, for Yahweh has refused them."

3. Yahweh and Jeremiah

The oracles reveal a side of Yahweh that Israel had a hard time accepting. What have you observed about Yahweh's attitude? The questions He asked in chapter 5 indicate something of the struggle of God to administer judgment. He doesn't want to bring destruction, but He says He has no choice.

Jeremiah also enters into that struggle. He can't understand what is going on. He lives in anguish as he anticipates the sounds of war. He finds himself proclaiming an unpopular message and one he finds no joy in giving. He tries to find exceptions 5:4, 5, but has to agree that there is no reason to withhold judgment.

4. Remnant

The concept of a remnant is mentioned in 6:9, but not developed as such. Throughout the predictions of devastation there are a few lines indicating limits of destruction. Note the refrain repeated in these verses:

4:27

5:10 _____

5:18 _____

There are several hints of the possibility of repentance, but the realistic picture is that Israel is beyond the point of return. Yet judgment is not viewed as the final end.

Summary

1. Characterizations

Decide on a few words that summarize what the section, 4:5—6:30, says about:

The people _____

Jeremiah _____

Yahweh _____

2. Consolidation

A good way to consolidate the fruit of study is to identify what you have discovered that is important to you in your understanding and obedience. What three observations or conclusions do you want to retain?

a. _____

b. _____

c. _____

Plan to share these with the study group.

3. Review of Chapters 1-6

Although the Book of Jeremiah does not follow a chronological order, these first six chapters seem to represent the early ministry of Jeremiah. They may reflect the prophet's ministry and message during the reign of Josiah. A short handle for each block will aid memory.

Chapter 1. _____

Chapter 2. Yahweh's Indictment of Israel

Chapter 3. Repentance

Chapters 4—6. _____

5. Jeremiah's Critique of Religion in Israel

Introduction

Focus. Another element of Jeremiah's message is found in oracles grouped with accounts of a "temple sermon." The issue was religion in Israel. Jeremiah criticized the religious practices and abuses of his day. We will study his critique of religion and what he said about worship, sacrifices, institutionalism, wisdom, idols, and vanities. Finally we want to discover what the message means for us today.

Scripture. Jeremiah 7—10; 26; 2 Kings 23:28-37.

Prayer. Yahweh God, You are the Lord of the nations, and the redeemer of Your people. Only with You is true power and wisdom. You are our Creator and the source of healing. Deliver us from false securities and from being drawn into the ways of the culture around us. Show us our inconsistencies and disobedience as we look into Jeremiah's message. We venture to ask that Jesus come and again cleanse the temple of His people. Thank you for Your Word. In Jesus name. Amen.

Review of the Times (2 Kings 23:28-37)

Jeremiah 26 is dated in the year of Jehoiakim's accession to the throne. That likely puts the time as 608 BC. Second Kings 23:28 ff. records the sequence of events.

1. Josiah was killed in battle.

    When? _____ Where? _____

    By whom? _____

2. Next king was _____

    Made king by _____ Length of reign was _____

3. Next king was (two names) _____ _____

    Made king by _____

    Judah now paying tribute to _____ (country)

4. In 605 BC Babylon took over

During Josiah's reign worship was centralized in Jerusalem. Outlying worship centers were closed with political reasons involved. More and more Jerusalem became the religious center for Judah even including the northern people. The reforms ended with Josiah, and so did the independence he had gained. With power shifting among the major nations, the political situation was unstable also in Judah. The temple continued to be a central shrine as pagan worship centers arose again.

The "Temple Sermon" (Two Accounts Compared)

Almost everyone agrees that Jeremiah 7:1-15 and 26:1-19 refer to the same occasion. Use the chart below to analyze the two accounts and to note the similarities and differences. Leave blanks where there is no information.

	7:1-15	26:1-19
Time		
Place		
Source of message		
Audience		
Purpose		
Sermon Points		
Sermon length (vv.)		
Response		

Why were the people so upset by Jeremiah's sermon that they were ready to lynch him?

Jeremiah's Trial

Although the chapter 26 account has only a brief summary of the sermon, it includes a detailed account of the trial which followed. The following outline will help you analyze that incident.

1. Problem: popular reaction to the temple sermon

Who reacted? _____

Mob verdict: _____

Why, what reasons given? _____

2. Court: duly authorized civil court, conducted by the princes

Charges brought: _____

3. Jeremiah's defense

Credentials: _____

Review of message: _____

Plea (v. 14): _____

Warning: _____

4. Verdict of the court: _____

5. Testimony of elders. To what part of the tradition did they appeal?

_____

6. Outcome (v. 24): _____

What is your evaluation of the trial? Any surprises?

Jeremiah's Critique of Religion in Israel

The following points are drawn primarily from Jeremiah 7—10.
1. Shallow repentance. (This came out in 3:1—4:4, Lesson 3.)
2. The temple had become central rather than the covenant God. The temple had become the center for a state-religion. Jeremiah asserted that trust in the temple was a lie (7:4) and that the only security was in obedience (26:4-6). You will recall that the Pharisess and Sadducees wanted their temple without wanting Jesus.
3. Worship was separated from right living (7:8-11). Israel saw no conflict between formal worship and immoral living. Who picked up the

reference to the temple as a "den of robbers" and on what occasion? (Mt. 21:13).

_____

How is moral insensitivity expressed in 8:12?

_____

4. When it ceases to direct people to God, a place of worship has no use. Jeremiah referred to Shiloh to prove the point. Shiloh was the location of the ark of the covenant and the tabernacle from the time of Joshua until the time of Samuel. What can you find out about Shiloh? Could it be that history lesson that riled the sermon hearers?

5. The externals of religion are no substitute for obedience. Note the strong emphasis on obedience in the sermon accounts. Another example is 9:25, 26. They were circumcised, but yet not circumcised (in heart).

6. Exposure of the folly of idols (10:1-16). There is really no comparison between Yahweh and idols because idols are worthless. List three of the reasons Jeremiah gave for not worshiping idols in 10:1-16.

a. _____

b. _____

c. _____

How does this assessment of idols fit the modern idolatries?

7. Mixing worship of the gods of the nations in with worship of Yahweh. The people did not intend to replace Yahweh with their idols. They only wanted to have both. But Yahweh will have none of it (7:16-20, 30-34).

8. Challenge to the "wise men" who were associated with the national policy. They trusted in the law (Torah) and went on to turn law into a lie (8:8). There are two kinds of wisdom. The kind Jeremiah criticized was the "sensible" wisdom, the kind Solomon could use to excuse intermarriage and recognition of other religions. The prophet says the only true wisdom is in trusting Yahweh. Wisdom cannot be separated from holy living (9:24). What New Testament passages sound like 9:23, 24?

_____

9. Critique of sacrifices and the sacrifice system (7:21-23). The meaning of 7:22 is found in the fact that sacrificing was already a part of their practice; God only told them how to do it. Verse 21 says that they might as well eat their sacrifices instead of completely burning them up. That way they would at least get some good out of them!

Sacrifices were a prominent part of Israelite worship. However, a critique of sacrifices runs through the Old Testament. Summarize the thrust of the following passages:

1 Samuel 15:22 _____

Micah 6:6-8 _____

Isaiah 1:10-17 _____

Amos 4:4, 5 _____

Amos 5:21-24 _____

Hosea 6:6 _____

Psalm 40:6-8 _____

Psalm 51:16, 17 _____

Proverbs 15:8 _____

What do you conclude is to be the place of sacrifice in Christian faith and worship?

Summary and Reflection

From the nine points of critique listed above, select four that seem to you to be major elements of Jeremiah's critique of religion in his time. (Perhaps you can combine several points in your summary list.)

1. _____

2. _____

3. _____

4. _____

If Jeremiah were here today, what do you think he would challenge with respect to the institutional church, worship patterns, and the practices of religion among Christians?

What needs to be central in worship? It is usually easier to list what is wrong than to state what ought to be. However, a lot of positive aspects have been stated or implied in the Scriptures reviewed in this lesson. Develop a positive group statement on worship that speaks to and for professing Christians today.

6. The Inner Turmoil of a Prophet

Introduction
　Focus. This lesson looks at scattered passages in chapters 11—20 that are the prophet's outcries to God. These "confessions" or complaints reveal much about the prophet and his reactions to the suffering that came with his vocation. It explores how we deal with doubts and bitterness arising out of life experiences.
　Scripture. Jeremiah 11:18-23; 12:1-6; 18:18-23; 20:7-18.
　Prayer. Lord, You are a God of infinite patience. You are not two-faced with us and we can be entirely open with You. We confess that we do not fully understand Your ways, but we thank You that we can come to You with the cries of our hearts even when we are torn apart with inner turmoil. Speak to us out of Jeremiah's experience and words for Your glory. Amen.

Confession and Lament Passages in Jeremiah
　Much of Jeremiah is made up of oracles of God spoken by the prophet to God's people. Some passages are narrative, describing events. A few passages in chapters 11—20 record the words of the prophet addressed to Yahweh. The oracles often voice God's complaint against His people, as in Lesson 3. But Jeremiah had his own complaints to register against God. He voiced his feelings about the treatment he received, about what God was not doing, and about his vocation as a prophet. These complaints are referred to as Jeremiah's "confessions." In addition to the four passages listed above for study in this lesson, similar material is found in 15:10-21; 17:14-18; and a few shorter passages.
　Read aloud with feeling the four Scripture selections for this lesson to get a feel for this type of material. What are your initial reactions?

_____

What do the passages have in common? List your observations.

_____

About one third of the psalms are individual or national laments. Look up

Psalm 44 or 74. Do you know other psalms that express similar feelings toward God?

___

What other Old Testament books are in a similar vein?

___

Review of Jeremiah's Experience of Life

1. Prediction at call (1:19): _____

2. Kind of message he had (2—10): _____

3. Marital status: _____ Why? (16:1-9) _____

4. How he was received (20:1, 2; 26:11): _____

5. A specific feeling response (8:18—9:1): _____

6. Instruction from Yahweh (7:16; 11:14; 14:11) _____

How do you imagine you would react to such a set of circumstances?

Four "Confessions" of Jeremiah

The following excerises will help you look more carefully at four of the "confessions." In each case you will be looking at what Jeremiah's problem was, how he reacted, and how Yahweh responded to him. Supply a title for each of the complaints.

(1) 11:18-23. _____

a. Jeremiah's problems:
"Now I find out they're plotting against me."
"I've come into this as innocent as _____." (v. 19).
"They want to cut me off so my name is no longer remembered." Denied marriage and family by Yahweh, he had already been denied posterity and name.

b. Jeremiah's reaction (describe): _____

___

___

c. Yahweh's answer (vv. 21-23): _____

___

(2) *12:1-6.* _____

    a. Jeremiah's problem (v. 1b): _____

    b. Jeremiah's reaction (Verse 1a is a lawcourt setting. A likely translation is):

        "You are innocent, Yahweh,
        when I file complaint against You;
        yet I will pass judgment on You."

William Holladay explains that Jeremiah is saying in effect: "God, you have been suing Israel for breach of contract, and I am your messenger in this regard. But when I undertook to be your messenger you obligated yourself to me to defend me, and you have not followed through on your obligation. Therefore get down from the judge's bench, move out from the prosecutor's stand, and take your place as a defendant so that *I* may sue *you* for breach of contract. Oh, I know, you will turn out to be innocent in the lawsuit between us; nevertheless I will have my day in court—I want to pass judgment upon you" (*Jeremiah: Spokesman Out of Time,* United Church Press, 1974).

Similar thoughts are expressed in Job 9.

    c. Yahweh's answer: "If you think you have problems now, cheer up, the worst is yet to come" (v. 5).

(3) *18:18-23.* _____

    a. Jeremiah's problems:

Verse 18. _____
Verse 20. "Where is justice?"
      "They are out to get me!" (Paranoia?)
      "I interceded for them, and what do I get?"
    b. Jeremiah's reactions (vv. 21-23). What does Jeremiah ask?

For children _____

For women _____

For men _____

For young men _____
How do you square Jeremiah's words with Matthew 5:38-48?
    c. Yahweh's answer: No answer.

(4) *20:7-18.* _____
    a. Jeremiah's problems:
A more explicit rendering of v. 7a is:

"Yahweh, you have seduced me,
 You have overpowered me and raped me."
Jeremiah was laughed at and mocked.
His message had become a reproach and derision.

What is his problem in v. 9?_____
"They are whispering and plotting all around me."
    b. Jeremiah's reactions:
Verses 11-13. Confidence of protection and deliverance.
Curses. (Just short of cursing God, mother, or father.)

Verse 14_____

Verse 15_____
"Why was I born?"
    c. Yahweh's answer: Any answer?_____ Any rebuke?_____ Why not?

How do you feel about Jeremiah's outbursts by this time?

____Judgmental. No one should talk to God that way.

____Sympathetic. I've felt that way at times myself.

____Embarrassed. Such passages in the Bible bother me.

____Encouraged. If Jeremiah could be honest, maybe I can, too.

____Perplexed. I don't see why Jeremiah was so upset.

____Angry. God didn't give Jeremiah much help.

____Other: _____

Summary Observations on Jeremiah's "Confessions"
    1. Jeremiah did not doubt God's existence, but he did question God's justice and timing.
    2. The complaints deal openly with doubt (as do many other Old Testament passages in Job and the psalms). Our hymnbooks do not have such honest laments in them as are found in the psalms. Should they have? What do you do with similar doubts?
    3. Jeremiah's laments are closely tied to his vocation as a prophet. His vocation led to suffering, and suffering led to inner struggles. These laments are the "cry of a man about the business of Yahweh." If we are obedient in our Christian calling and mission, there may well be suffering. Attention needs to be fixed on vocation, not the suffering.

4. The complaints passages make some of us uncomfortable. Why? May it be that we have not yet come to terms with our own feelings?
5. The passages of this lesson reveal the humanness of the prophet.
6. Record your personal discoveries:

About Jeremiah: _____

_____

About God: _____

_____

About life: _____

_____

About yourself: _____

_____

The third play in *Judgment and Hope,* by John W. Miller (Herald Press, 1972), is about "Jeremiah's Dark Night of the Soul."

7. Jeremiah's Message Dramatized and Symbolized

Introduction

Focus. This lesson is concerned with how Jeremiah communicated his message as well as with what that message was. At Yahweh's direction Jeremiah experienced and used a number of symbolic actions throughout his ministry. We will look at six of these and the message they communicated.

Scripture. Jeremiah 13:1-11; 16:1-9; 18:1-12; 19:1-15; 20:1-6; 27:1-15; (32:1-15; 35).

Prayer. Our Lord and God, how marvelous are Your ways. You speak to us in so many ways. You must know that we sometimes need vivid drama and pictures to understand what You are saying. Thank you for providing symbolic actions as well as just plain words in the Bible. Bless us in our study of Jeremiah so that we are led to know and do more fully Your will. In the name of Jesus we pray. Amen.

Extra-verbal Elements in Jeremiah.

How does a prophet communicate Yahweh's message to a people slow of hearing and understanding? Primarily the prophets spoke in verbal oracles, but not exclusively. A number of "unusual actions" of the prophets are found in the Old Testament. These acted parables or symbolic actions are what may be called "extra-verbal" or "para-verbal."

Examples are the arrow Elisha had Joash shoot in the direction of Syria (2 Kings 13:14 ff.), Hosea's marriage experiences, Isaiah's going naked and barefoot (Is. 20), and Ezekiel's laying on his side. There are many such acted messages in Jeremiah. These were not magical or spectacular enactments to call attention to the prophet himself, but a means of driving home a particular point of the prophet's message or prediction. They are integral with the message of the prophet from Yahweh. Often the contribution is to emphasize the certainty of the spoken word.

Survey of the Acted Parables

The intent here is to become familiar with the circumstances and details of these parables and then with the aid of a few notes of explanation to state the meaning they had and have. Plan to share observations and questions with the study group.

1. *The Linen Waistcloth That Was Spoiled (13:1-11)*
   a. Summarize what Jeremiah did, and what the outcome was.

   _____

   _____

   _____

   b. Notes. The garment mentioned was worn next to the body. Notice that Jeremiah wore this one, but was not to wash it. It should not be ruled out that Jeremiah actually made two trips to the Euphrates, which was about 250 miles one way. The explanation came to him after he did what he was told to do. No mention is made of bringing the waistcloth back again. The explanation in verses 8-11 makes the basic elements of the parable clear, and we do well not to push the details beyond the interpretation Yahweh gave.
   c. State the meaning of the parable in your own words.

   _____

   _____

2. *Jeremiah's Celebate and Restricted Life (16:1-9)*
   a. Summarize the restrictions placed on Jeremiah.

   _____

   _____

   b. Notes. Jeremiah did not advocate that no one get married. His own celebacy and other restrictions were a sign of the way life would be in the coming doom. His solitary life was an object lesson to the people.
   c. State the meaning of this parable in your own words.

   _____

   _____

3. *The Potter and the Clay (18:1-12)*
   a. Summarize what Jeremiah witnessed at the potter's house.

   _____

   _____

   b. Notes. The object lesson leaves no doubt but that God is the divine potter. But although the clay and pot represent God's people, in a real sense people and nations are not clay. They can change. In its setting this acted parable is about the nation of Judah, not about individual persons. What do you find these verses saying about God's sovereignty? What does it say about the freedom of a people?

    c. State the meaning of the parable in your own words.

_____

_____

_____

4. *Breaking a Flask at the Gate of the City (19:1-15)*
    a. Summarize the action reported, noting what, who, and where.

_____

_____

_____

    b. Notes. This is a hardened flask, not a soft one that can be remade. Not just an ordinary pot, this flask had value to its owner. The place where Jeremiah broke the flask is significant. The Valley of Hinnom was to the south of Jerusalem and could be viewed from the Potsherd Gate. That was the place of dumping refuse and also the location on the sacrificing of children (vv. 5, 6). Among the witnesses were the priests who plotted against Jeremiah (18:18). Imagine in your mind the intense drama of that day.

    c. State the meaning of the parable in your own words.

_____

_____

_____

5. *Renaming a High-Ranking Priest (20:1-6)*
    a. Summarize the action including what Pashhur did to Jeremiah and what Jeremiah did the next morning.

_____

_____

_____

    b. Notes. Jeremiah, whom God appointed "overseer" (1:10), was openly persecuted by the "overseer" of the temple. Jeremiah announced that Pashhur was to have a new name, "Terror on every side." That term occurs in Jeremiah 6:25; 20:10; 46:5; and 49:29. The meaning of Pashhur is not clear, but the meaning of the new name is explained by what Jeremiah said. Notice in verse 6 why Pashhur was given this judgment.

    c. State the meaning of this symbolic action.

6. *Wearing an Ox-Yoke (27:1-15)*
   a. Summarize what Jeremiah did, before whom, and when.

   b. Notes. The wooden yoke-bar with leather thongs to tie around the animal's neck or to its horns was the common ox-yoke. The message with the symbolic action was given to envoys of five surrounding nations. Zedekiah also got the message. Notice what Nebuchadnezzar is called in verse 6. Was the yoke of Babylon a symbol of life or of death? Note when this took place.
   c. State the meaning of this symbolic act.

   Another symbolic action is told about in 32:1-15. Nebuchadnezzar's army was attacking Jerusalem. While Jeremiah was in custody of the king he had opportunity to purchase a piece of family property in Anathoth. Buying real estate while predicting the defeat of Judah was either insanity or a way of putting the message of hope in tangible form. Read the story for yourself.
   An example of Jeremiah's creative communication appears in chapter 35. Jeremiah invited some Rechabites to a banquet and then offered them wine, which he knew was totally contrary to their tradition. He then used their refusal to drink wine to preach against the loss of conviction and faithfulness in Judah.

Summarization
   1. How many of the acted parables can you recall without looking at the lesson materials or Bible?
   2. What was the nature of the message Jeremiah delivered by and with the aid of action parables? Which of them carried a message of judgment, and which a message of hope? Why do you think Yahweh had him use these methods?
   3. What have you learned about Jeremiah as a person in these accounts?
   4. Brainstorm some creative ways to communicate the message you are getting from Jeremiah. Try to get the message and the medium to converge.
   Plays 1 and 5 in *Judgment and Hope* include some of the incidents of this lesson.

8. Jeremiah's Oracles on Kingship

Introduction

Focus. This lesson considers kings and the meaning of kingship in Judah. Jeremiah had something to say about each of the five kings who were on the throne of David in Jerusalem during the time of his ministry. In addition to Jeremiah's attitude toward specific kings, we have opportunity to pick up his views about the monarchy in the ongoing purpose of God. Of particular interst will be the contribution of three messianic oracles to an understanding of kingship.

Scripture. Jeremiah 21:1—23:8.

Prayer. Yahweh God, You are King. We've often said that, but in this study we seek to know what kind of King You are. Because Jeremiah spoke Your message about kings we can know You better. Thank you for instructing us through the Word. Amen.

The Last Five Kings of Judah

Let's get some basic facts in mind about the kings of Judah during the time of Jeremiah, beginning with Josiah. Refer to 2 Kings 23:24—24:20; Jeremiah 22:11, 24; and the list of kings and events in Lesson 1 of this study for the needed information. (See also 1 Chronicles 3:15, 16.)

Personal Name	Throne Name	Father's Name	Age Enthroned	Length of Reign	Assessment (Good or Evil)
_____	_____	_____	_____	_____	_____
_____	_____	_____	_____	_____	_____
_____	_____	_____	_____	_____	_____
_____	_____	_____	_____	_____	_____
_____	_____	_____	_____	_____	_____

(In the parallel account in 2 Chronicles, the reference to "brother" in

36:10 needs to be taken in the sense of brother of Jehoiakim, or changed to uncle.)

An Incident during the Reign of Zedekiah (21:1-10)

As arranged in the Book of Jeremiah, the first oracle about kings has to do with the last king of Judah, Zedekiah. The material in the chapters preceding 21 contains very little reference to definite events or persons that can be dated. However, 21:1-10 is dated in the reign of Zedekiah, and very likely describes an incident about the time when the siege of Jerusalem was beginning. The three paragraphs are about a request, an answer, and a message about two ways.

1. Zedekiah's Request

Note that the king treated the prophet with respect, and as a help for securing the favor of Yahweh. What was Zedekiah's request (in your words)?

_____

More than a century before, king Hezekiah had sent to the prophet Isaiah with a similar request for Yahweh's intervention, and the answer was favorable (2 Kings 19:1-7; Is. 37:1-7). Perhaps Zedekiah reasoned: "Yahweh did it before, He can do it again."

2. Yahweh's Answer Through Jeremiah

The answer was not what the king hoped for. Yahweh would fight against Jerusalem. The prediction is twofold:

Concerning Jerusalem the prediction is _____

Concerning the king and people it is _____

3. The Two Ways

Jeremiah 21:8 is set in language similar to Deuteronomy 30:19. See also Deuteronomy 11:26. Reference to choice, two ways, life and death, is covenant language. In Deuteronomy it is a matter of obedience or disobedience in the covenant relationship. In Jeremiah the application is a bit different, although not separated from covenant. According to 21:8-10,

the way of death is to _____

and the way of life is to_____

That seemingly contradictory and unpopular advice became the consistent message of Jeremiah as the end approached.

It should be noted in passing that there is a striking similarity between some of Jeremiah's oracles and the emphasis of Deuteronomy on covenant. The specific parallel of the two ways is only one example. Jeremiah shares the theology of Deuteronomy.

Oracles to the Dynasty of David (21:11—22:9)

Several general oracles precede messages to specific kings. Note that they are addressed to "the house of David," "the king of Judah who sits on the throne of David," "the house of the king of Judah." The prophet had something to say to the dynasty of David. The word of Yahweh to the royal house of Judah had to do with requirements and judgment.

1. Requirements

Covenant brings privileges, but also brings responsibilities. What Yahweh expects and requires is justice and righteousness, and doing something about oppression.

Find two verses that express these basic covenant requirements.

21:_____   22:_____

The same emphasis appears in the message to the kings, for example, 22:13-17.

2. Judgment

In 21:11-14 the message is a warning to repent to avoid Yahweh's wrath. In 22:4, 5 the pattern is "if . . . but if not. . . ." However, the oracles conclude with a certainty of judgment. What reason is given for the desolation of the house of David in 22:9?

_____

What arguments would likely have been given in defense of the dynasty of David? What false hopes made Jeremiah's advice and predictions unacceptable?

Oracles Concerning Specific Kings (22:10-30)

The three kings following Josiah are each included, in order. Josiah is not mentioned by name but is referred to favorably in 22:10, 15-16.

1. Concerning Shallum [Jehoahaz] (22:10-12)

The oracles concerning Jehoahaz, who reigned only three months before being exiled, are in the nature of a lament that he is gone, never to return again. For reasons we do not know about, he was the people's choice ahead of his older brothers.

2. Concerning Jehoiakim (22:13-19)

Of all the kings to whom Jeremiah related, Jehoiakim gave the prophet the most trouble. In spite of difficult times Jehoiakim expanded his luxury with forced labor. He disregarded the needs of people. Yet to do something about the poor and needy is to know Yahweh, 22:16. Jeremiah predicted that there would not be any lamenting over the death of this king.

Verses 20-23 speak of the doom of Jerusalem and the shepherds (kings).

3. Concerning Coniah [Jehoiachin] (22:24-30)

The message predicts the exile of this king and his mother, without return. Jehoiachin's deportation with his mother after only three months on the throne is recorded in 2 Kings 24:8 ff. Verse 30 says Jehoiachin's obituary can record him as childless. Although he had seven sons (1 Chron. 3:17 f.) none succeeded him to the throne of David.

The dynasty of David was about to terminate. Jehoahaz would never return. Jehoiakim would be thrown out like a dead animal. Jehoiachin would never return. One more king came on the scene, but his line didn't continue either. Yet as the next oracles announce, the end of the kings was not the end of God's provision for His people.

Why was Israel's detour into kingship a bad choice from the start? Review what Yahweh said through Samuel about the monarchy venture, 1 Samuel 8.

Three Messianic Oracles (23:1-8)

Although the term "Messiah" does not appear in the passage, there is little doubt that the oracles point to the Messiah as the true Shepherd/King who will be what the dynasty of David failed to be.

1. Shepherds

The term "shepherd" commonly carries the meaning of king in the Old Testament (and as Jesus applied it to Himself). So the woe pronounced on the shepherds is directed to the kings and rulers. Zedekiah and his nobles are likely in mind. Using the shepherd figure, the oracle accuses the king of destroying and scattering the flock instead of doing what rulers are supposed to do. Because of the failure of the ruler they will be replaced with true shepherds, who care for the people.

2. A Righteous Branch of David

The oracle in verses 5 and 6 builds on a similarity and a contrast. The name Zedekiah means "Yahweh is righteous." The new messianic King will be called "Yahweh is our righteousness." Zedekiah had a good name, but he was not true to his name. He was a weakling. In contrast the new King will execute justice and righteousness in the land. The new King will be all that the old line was supposed to be but wasn't. Then Israel will have safety and security, descriptive of true shalom.

3. New Exodus

A deliverance is envisioned that will far outdo Israel's redemption from Egypt, which was the model of God's redemptive power. The new exodus will bring the descendants of the exiles back again. That makes the Messiah greater than Moses.

What do the kings of Judah and the Messiah have in common?

What is the main contrast between the kings of Judah and the Messiah?

Summary Observations

At this point you may be asking, what is the point of combing through what Jeremiah said about the kings of his time? Maybe it appears to be as exciting as a lecture on the good and bad points of wooden wheels on a chariot to a fellow ready to board a jetliner for Tokyo. The connecting links to our experience are not as obvious as they were in lessons on repentance and worship. Whether Israel had kings or not, and how they turned out may not have a direct bearing on our lives this week, but for an understanding of the Old Testament and of Jesus' place in the life of His people today the oracles on kingship are relevant and instructive.

As a way of summarizing the relevance of this study, test the following observations against the fruit of your own study and the group discussion. Write in what you sense to be the significance of these summary points in the blanks on the right. Add any other observations you have.

1. As the prophet of Yahweh, Jeremiah can criticize the kings of Israel for their failures.

2. Judgment fell on the house of David because of failing in the covenant responsibilities of justice, righteousness, and concern for the poor and oppressed.

3. Although elements in the Old Testament are favorable to kingship, Jeremiah and other prophets are critical of the monarchy.

4. Although promised a permanent throne, the dynasty of David came to an end after 400 years.

5. The high point of Bible history is not the kingdom of David and his successors, but the Christ on the cross, risen and ascended.

6. The Messiah-Shepherd is in the tradition of Moses (as much or more than in the tradition of David) with the power of the "word of Yahweh."

7. True peace is not through kings with armies, but through the Messiah who is a different kind of king.

Part of play 5 in *Judgment and Hope* is about the incident in 21:1-10.

9. Jeremiah's Oracles on Prophets

Introduction
Focus. Jeremiah was not the only prophet in his time. The oracles about prophets which we give attention to in this lesson grow out of intense personal encounters experienced by Jeremiah. The issue of false and true prophets directly involved Jeremiah. His grappling with the issue provides some help for us in discerning who the true and false prophets are in our time.

Scripture. Jeremiah 23:9-40; 27—29.

Prayer. Father God, we believe You are truth and not falsehood. You have Your true prophets, but there are also prophets who proclaim lies. We seek to know how to discern true prophets through the experiences and message of Jeremiah. For this we need the enlightenment of the Holy Spirit. Thank you. Amen.

A Problem: Is the Prophet True or False?
It isn't easy to tell for sure who the true prophets are. It wasn't an easy matter in Jeremiah's time, and it isn't now. When we read of false prophets in the Bible we may forget that nobody goes around wearing a tag identifying himself as a false prophet. Every prophet claims to be a true prophet.

The ultimate test of a prophet is whether his predictions come true, (Deut. 18:22). That is all right for hindsight, but not much help for the present. Waiting to find out if the prophecy comes true may make it too late to act on the message. The true prophet is in the best position to know who is true. But it is the people who need to know in the midst of claims and counter-claims. Jeremiah had his own integrity challenged, yet he stuck to his claim to be a prophet of Yahweh. The passages included in this lesson provide a number of clues as to how Jeremiah resolved the issue. We will be on the lookout for criteria for distinguishing between true and false prophets.

General Oracles Concerning Prophets (23:9-40)
1. Observing the Text

Notice that these oracles are not dated.

How many occurrences of "prophet" or "prophets" do you find? _____

To whom are the oracles addressed? _____

_____

2. *Specific Accusations against (False) Prophets*

Note the charge(s) Yahweh brings against prophets in the verses indicated.

Verse 11 _____

Verse 13 _____

Verse 14 _____

Verse 15 _____

Verse 16 _____

Verse 17 _____

Verse 18 _____

Verse 21 _____

Verse 25 _____

Verse 27 _____

Verse 30 _____

Verse 31 _____

Verse 36 _____

Star one or two that seem to you to carry the most weight.

3. *Explanatory Notes*

The mention in 23:18 of "the council of Yahweh" has special meaning for the true prophet. Jeremiah is saying that the true prophet gets his message by listening in on the council of Yahweh when the heavenly court is assembled. He is present, as it were, when the decisions are made. The false prophet has no such source for his message. He borrows, he dreams, he talks when he has not been told what to say.

The last paragraph, 33-40, rests on a turn of words. Apparently a way of greeting a prophet was to ask him, "What is the burden of Yahweh?" Yahweh told Jeremiah that when he is asked that question he is to say, "You are the burden of Yahweh, a burden to be cast off."

Specific Messages Concerning Prophets (27:1-22)

The story of chapters 27, 28, and 29 is dated early in Zedekiah's reign; 28:1 ties 27 and 28 together in the fourth year of Zedekiah, (Refer to the list of kings and events in Lesson 1, if you need to, to get your bearing.) The name Zedekiah needs to be used in 27:1 to agree with verse 3. Notice that the account in chapter 27 is told in first person ("Yahweh said to me," "I said").

Zedekiah went to Babylon during his fourth year (51:59). Whether it was his own idea or he was summoned by Nebuchadnezzar is not known. In chapter 27 representatives of five nations met with Zedekiah in Jerusalem, possibly to form an alliance of resistance against Babylon. That high-level conference was the occasion for Jeremiah to speak for Yahweh.

1. Message to Five Kings (27:1-11)

Jeremiah's use of the symbolic yoke has already been included in Lesson 7. We will return to this passage again in the next lesson because of what it says to the nations. Our interest here is in what is said about prophets. That warning is:

"Do not listen to your prophets, your diviners, your dreamers, your soothsayers, or your sorcerers, who are saying to you, 'You shall not serve the king of Babylon.' For it is a lie which they are prophesying to you" (27:9-10a).

2. Message to Zedekiah (27:12-15)

The warning about the prophets of Judah is essentially the same:

"Do not listen to the words of the prophets who are saying to you, 'You shall not serve the king of Babylon,' for it is a lie which they are prophesying to you" (27:14).

3. Message to the Priests and All the People (27:16-22)

A related prediction of the false prophets comes out in this message. When the previous king, Jehoiachin, had been deported to Babylon some of the temple vessels and treasures had been taken along. That had been four years previous to this message:

"Do not listen to the words of your prophets who are prophesying to you, saying, 'Behold, the vessels of the Lord's house will now shortly be brought back from Babylon,' for it is a lie which they are prophesying to you" (27:16)

Underline the common elements in these three messages. How do you suppose the prophets of Judah felt about being classed with the prophets and sorcerers of the surrounding nations? For additional study, note the results of listening to the false prophets: verses 8, 10, 13, 15, 17b, and the results of listening to Yahweh: verses 11, 12, 17a.

Prophet Versus Prophet: Confrontation with Hananiah (28:1-17)

The chapter records a dramatic encounter between Jeremiah and a prophet named Hananiah, who claimed to be a messenger from Yahweh. As you consider the episode decide if you think Hananiah was self-deceived or knew full-well that his message was not from Yahweh.

1. Hananiah's Prophecy (vv. 1-4)

Where and before whom?(v.1) _____

For whom was Hananiah speaking? (v.2) _____

He announced the breaking of the yoke of the king of Babylon, with two results in two years. What were those predictions?

_____

_____

_____

2. Jeremiah's Response (vv. 5-9)
   Jeremiah made a public reply. His "Amen" was like saying, "I wish it could be that way." He went on to point out that it is not in the tradition of the prophets to preach peace. Yet it is not necessary to be a prophet of doom to be a true prophet. The issue is the basis of peace. Hananiah had no basis for predicting peace at that time. Jeremiah cautiously resorted to the fulfillment test, verse 9.

3. Hananiah's Rejoinder (vv. 10-11)
   Jeremiah had been wearing yoke-bars on his neck (27:2). Hananiah reinforced his prediction of the end of Nebuchadnezzar's domination of the nation in two years by taking Jermiah's yoke-bars and breaking them. Notice Jeremiah's reaction at the end of verse 11. If Jeremiah had kept a diary, what do you suppose he wrote that night?

_____

_____

_____

4. Jeremiah's Further Word from Yahweh (vv. 12-17)
   After some time Jeremiah got his answer. With respect to Nebuchadnezzar, the figure of the yoke-bars was changed from wood to iron. And there was a message to Hananiah. What was he guilty of, according to verses 15 and 16?

_____

   How do you feel about his sentence?

_____

Jeremiah's Correspondence with the Exiles (29:1-32)
   Chapter 29 is of special interest for at least two reasons. The fact that it records the text of three letters between Jerusalem and Babylon is exciting in itself. Further it gives us additional material on Jeremiah's dealings with the other prophets and God's evaluation of them.

1. *First Letter to the Exiles in Babylon (vv. 1-23)*

Note the detailed information as to who received the letter from Jeremiah and how and when it got to Babylon. Jeremiah was accused of being pessimistic, of being a prophet of doom, and of demoralizing the people. But the letter is basically a message of hope and good news. Summarize the elements of good news and bad news in the letter.

Good News	Bad News
_____	_____
_____	_____
_____	_____

2. *Shemaiah's Letter about Jeremiah (vv. 24-28)*

Shemaiah's letter to the priest of Jerusalem, Zephaniah, reveals how Jeremiah's letter had been received. The exiles didn't want to hear anything about building houses and planting gardens. They wanted to go back to Jerusalem. Shemaiah wrote to have Jeremiah silenced.

3. *Jeremiah's Second Letter to Babylon (vv. 29-32)*

The priest read the letter to Jeremiah, but did not put him in stocks. Jeremiah's letter of reply in the name of Yahweh spelled out Shemaiah's sentence for his prophecies. Record the offenses he was guilty of.

a. _____

b. _____

c. _____

Causing People to Trust a Lie

The Hebrew word translated "lie" occurs thirty-six times in Jeremiah. Fourteen of those are in the oracles about prophets included in this lesson. The primary charge against false prophets is that they speak lying words and cause people to trust in a lie. You may want to trace this concept as it stands out in the parts of Jeremiah examined in this lesson: 23:14, 25, 26, 32; 27:10, 14, 15, 16; 28:15; 29:9, 21, 23, 31.

The lie being promoted by the prophets opposed to Jeremiah was the popular nationalistic theology. On the one hand it was the blind optimism and false security that nothing would ever happen to God's people or the city of Jerusalem. On the other hand it was a profound doubt that God would or could help them, which resulted in turning to other sources of protection.

Jeremiah saw beyond the narrow confines of nationalism to God's long-range purposes. He could see the situation from the perspective of covenant. The lies of the other prophets destroyed covenant relationships and the reality of community that goes with covenant.

Criteria for Spotting False or True Prophets

Summarize your study by assembling a list of checkpoints for deciding whether a prophet is speaking God's message. Include points that are relevant for discernment today. Refine the list in the group.

_____

_____

_____

_____

_____

What need is there to discern true and false prophets today? What common elements are there between Jeremiah's times and ours? What differences complicate the discernment of prophets now? What additional resources do we have?

10. Prophecies to the Nations

Introduction

Focus. One distinct section of Jeremiah is the six-chapter collection of prophecies about the nations associated with Israel. One might ask, "Who cares what Jeremiah said about Ammon?" We don't know any Ammonites, and what happened to them in ancient times seems remote from our interests. But if we are concerned with the place of God in history, then these chapters and related passages in Jeremiah become important. Of special interest in this lesson about the nations will be (a) references to Nebuchadnezzar as the servant of Yahweh, (b) comparison of 25:15 ff. with 26—51, and (c) the implication of messages concerning certain nations. Of ultimate concern will be what God's role is in the coming and going of nations and what that means for the people of God today.

Scripture. Jeremiah 25:15-38; 46:1—51:64; and scattered passages.

Prayer. How big You are, God! Forgive us for thinking of You in limiting ways. We need the security of Your lordship. We also need to know what Your place is in history in a mixed-up world. Again we look to Jeremiah for a word from You. We praise You through Jesus our Lord, Amen.

"Concerning the Nations"

The preface to the prophecies in chapters 46—51 reads, "The word of the Lord which came to Jeremiah the prophet concerning the nations." In the study of Jeremiah's call we observed that God had appointed him prophet to the nations (1:5), and set him over nations and over kingdoms (1:10). It is not surprising, therefore, to find Jeremiah receiving a word from Yahweh concerning the nations. Jeremiah is not at all unique among the prophets in giving attention to other nations. Most of the prophets do that. Obadiah, for example, is almost exclusively directed toward Edom.

In 27:3-11 (Lesson 9) we found Jeremiah sending a message to the kings of five nations. That message was regarding Nebuchadnezzar and went to Edom, Moab, Ammon, Tyre, and Sidon. It seems fairly certain that that message was delivered. We have no clear indication whether the prophecies to the nations in 46—51 were ever actually delivered, nor is there evidence that they were not delivered to the respective nations. At any rate the message had as much to say to Israel as to the several nations.

Scholars are much interested in the fact that the Septuagint (Greek Old

Testament) has chapters 46—51 immediately following 25:13. The material of the six chapters is also in a different order. This difference suggests that the collection of oracles had a separate existence before being incorporated into the Book of Jeremiah as we now have it.

"Nebuchadnezzar, My Servant"

Nebuchadnezzar's name is prominent in the Book of Jeremiah. An alternate spelling, Nebuchadrezzar, is found in twenty-seven of the thirty-seven times this king of Babylon is mentioned in chapters 21—52. Of special interest is how he is identified in three places:

25:9, Nebuchadrezzar, _____, _____

27:6, Nebuchadrezzar, _____, _____

43:10, Nebuchadrezzar, _____, _____

In Jeremiah, the term servant is applied to Israel, Jacob, David, the prophet, and Nebuchadnezzar. For the God of Israel to call the king of Babylon "my servant" stretched, if not broke, Israel's framework for thinking. Although identified as the God of Israel, He is not presented in these passages as the God of redemption, but as Creator and Yahweh of hosts.

A major barrier for Israel, or any of the nations, to conceive of Yahweh as Lord of the nations was the tendency to connect the destiny of their king and nation with the strength of the national deity. For example, it would have been commonly interpreted that Nebuchadnezzar's defeat of Jerusalem meant that Babylon's gods were better than Israel's God. Similarly, Israel would have assumed that for Yahweh to call Nebuchadnezzar "my servant" implied that he approved of the Babylonian gods. But not so. Yahweh can be God of Israel at the same time he makes use of the king of Babylon for His larger purposes.

Paul, in similar language, referred to "Caesar" (and all rulers) as God's servant (Rom. 13:4). Jeremiah can help us understand Paul. What contribution does Jeremiah's interpretation of Nebuchadnezzar's role make to an understanding of Romans 13 and the relation of the church to "Caesar"?

Prophecies to Certain Nations

The first step in getting acquainted with the prophecies to the nations is to compare the list of nations in 25:15 ff. with the list in 46—51. On the left is the list as found in chapter 25. Fill in the blanks on the right, using the references.

Jerusalem, Judah

Egypt _____ 46:2-26

Uz (associated with Edom)

Philistines ——————————————47:1-7

Edom (Esau) ——————————————48:1-47

Moab (Lot) ——————————————49:1-6

Ammon (Lot) ——————————————49:7-22

Tyre

Sidon

——————————————49:23-27

Dedan ⎫
      ⎬ (Arabian tribes)
Tema ⎭

Buz (desert tribe?)

Arabia ——————————————49:28-33

Zimri (unknown)

Elam ——————————————49:34-39

Media

"North"

Sheshach (Babylon) ——————————————50:1—51:64

Note that the order is different for Edom, Moab, and Ammon in the two lists.
Kedar and Hazor stand for Arabia in 49:28-33.
Damascus (Syria) had not had independence for some time.
A concealed name for Babylon is found in the Hebrew of 25:26, Sheshach.
Elam, in both lists, is on the far side of Babylon, farthest from Jerusalem,
but neighbor to the Babylonian exiles.
Mark the five nations listed in 27:3.

    On the map on page 61 circle the nations that are the objects of oracles in Chapters 46—51 (the right-hand list).
    As a minimal survey of the messages to the nations, look for two elements in the nine oracles of chapters 46—51. Summarize in a few words the message

of doom and the message of hope, if any, for each of the nations in the chart below.

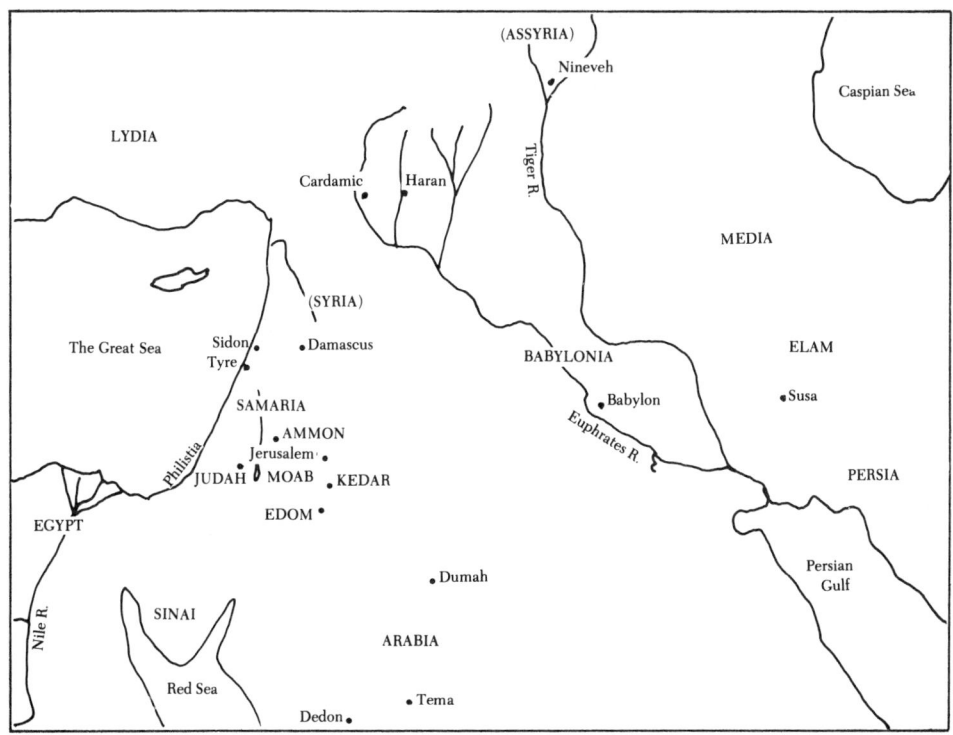

	Doom	**Hope**
Egypt	_____	_____
Philistines	_____	_____
Moab	_____	_____
Ammon	_____	_____
Edom	_____	_____
Damascus	_____	_____
Kedar/Hazor	_____	_____
Elam	_____	_____
Babylon	_____	_____

Consider the impact of these oracles on the people of Judah. While on the one hand many of the surrounding nations were traditional enemies for which doom would be cheered, several of them were also possible sources of help against Babylon. The oracles say there will be no help from Egypt. The Philistines will not be able to turn Nebuchadnezzar's armies back. There is no use looking to Elam for quick release from Babylonian exile.

Yahweh stands in judgment of the gods of these nations. A number of them are mentioned by name and pronounced useless. In Egypt it was Apis, the sacred bull, in Moab, Chemosh, in Ammon, Milcom (Molech). In Babylon, Marduk was the chief god, with the names of Merodach and Bel also used. How could a people who thought their God was failing them because Nebuchadnezzar was defeating Judah and taking the people captive be assured by a message of the helplessness of the foreign gods?

As the end for Jerusalem approached, Jeremiah consistently announced that Yahweh had given into the hand of Nebuchadnezzar not only Judah but all the nations. It is little wonder that the people thought Jeremiah had sold out to Babylon. Only for a time was Babylon to be on top of the pile. The longest prophecy is against Babylon. The end and desolation of mighty Babylon is also predicted. The hammer will also be smashed (50:23). Jeremiah arranged for a symbolic act to reinforce the message of Babylon's sinking to rise no more (51:59-64). Yet the predicted doom of Babylon did not alter the fact that Israel would be in Babylonian captivity for seventy years.

Yahweh as the "I" of History

What do these oracles about the nations say about Yahweh Himself? For one thing Yahweh is not as provincial as Israel was. They could not think of their God beyond their national boundaries. But He is bigger than that. The false prophets held to a narrow nationalism. Jeremiah, along with other prophets of Israel, recognized Yahweh's dominion over the nations. See Isaiah 2:1-4 and the refrain of Ezekiel, "Then they will know that I am Yahweh" (35:15, for example).

Yahweh alone is left saying "I." He could use Nebuchadnezzar as a "servant" yet not relinquish His place as God of Israel. Look through the Scriptures of this lesson for places where Yahweh said "I . . . " through Jeremiah. Record six such statements as a sampling of the dominant note of Yahweh's lordship.

Summary and Integration

Whether you remember the names and locations of all the nations to whom Jeremiah spoke the word of Yahweh is not terribly important. But you should not leave this lesson without reflecting on your own view of history and nations "under God." As a way of pulling your thoughts together, write a few lines about what it means to you in your own country that Yahweh is the "I" of history, and a few lines about what you sense the message is for Christian brothers and sisters in South Africa, the Middle East, or China. Plan to share your thoughts with the study group.

_____

_____

_____

_____

_____

_____

_____

11. The Book of Consolation

Introduction

Focus. Jeremiah was a prophet of hope as well as a prophet of doom. His message of hope is found in many scattered passages, but is primarily concentrated in what is commonly called "the Book of Consolation." Our study will deal with what Jeremiah's message of hope was, with special attention focused on what he said about a "new covenant." We will be concerned with the correlation of the oracles of hope with the rest of Jeremiah's message, and the connection between Jeremiah's words and other Old Testament covenants, and the New Testament fulfillment in Christ.

Scripture. Jeremiah 30—33 (also 1—10; 24; 29)

Prayer. Lord God and Father, You are a God of love and mercy. In the midst of despair You speak of deliverance and hope. To those experiencing the judgment of exile You speak of return. You promise a miracle that remakes and rebuilds Your people. As we search into a portion of Your Word, open our eyes to see You afresh and to rejoice as recipients ourselves of Your new blessings. In the name of Jesus we come with thanksgiving. Amen.

"The Book of Consolation"

"The Book of Consolation" is a distinct section of the larger collection of the Book of Jeremiah. As you look through Jeremiah 30 to 33 you will notice that these chapters are made up of a number of short oracles. The disjointedness at places finds explanation in its being a collection of messages. The four chapters are made up of two smaller units, 30—31 and 32—33. In translations that recognize poetry you will notice that 30—31 are mostly in poetry form, and 32—33 are almost entirely prose.

One outstanding feature, especially of 30—31, is the frequency of the phrase, "says the Lord" (literally, "utterance of Yahweh"). The fact that the section is made up of a number of shorter oracles may in part explain the repetition of this characteristic phrase. But the repeated punctuation with "utterance of Yahweh" serves to impress the reader with the source and weight of the oracles.

How many times does "says the Lord" occur in 30—31? _____

All four chapters have the common theme of hope beyond judgment. Five times we find the phrase, "Behold, the days are coming." There are other references to "the days" and "those days." While you look through the material for these references to the future, note also the many instances of future tense language ("they shall" and "I will"). This is clearly predictive prophecy.

Chapters 32 and 33 are dated (in the first verses) in the final siege of Jerusalem. Chapters 30 and 31 are undated. Evidence indicates that Jeremiah injected the message of hope at those times in Israel's experience when things looked the darkest.

Other Hope Passages in Jeremiah
Clear tones of hope sound forth in these three passages:

1. Jeremiah's Call (1:10)
Two of the six elements of Jeremiah's commission are positive.

Note the way the wording of 1:10 is repeated in 31:28.

2. The Vision of Good and Bad Figs (24)
The bad figs were the people of Judah who stayed and suffered destruction. The good figs were the exiles from Judah whom Yahweh said He would bring back again. Read 24:6, 7, noting correlations with 1:10 and 31:33.

3. Jeremiah's Letter to the Exiles (29:4ff.)
Note the significance of the wording in verse 5. Verse 11 speaks of a future and a hope. Verse 17 picks up the figure of figs again.

Outline of "the Book of Consolation"
The following outline does not provide a label for all of the sections of the four chapters, but should help you see the general structure and content. Use it as a guide for familiarizing yourself with this collection of messages of hope.

Introduction to the Collection, 30:1-3
I. Yahweh's Promises, 30:4—31:40

    A. No full end for Yahweh's people, 30:4-11
    B. Healing of incurable wounds, 30:12-17
    C. Restoration for Zion, 30:18-22
    D. God of all families of Israel, 30:23—31:1
    E. Homecoming for northern Israel, 31:2-14
    F. Rachel's lament for Ephraim and Yahweh's response, 31:15-20
    G. Yahweh's new thing, 31:21, 22
    H. Replenishing and rebuilding for Israel and Judah, 31:23-30
    I. The new covenant, 31:31-34
    J. The permanence of Israel and the city, 31:35-40

II. Yahweh's Sign, 32
    A. Jeremiah imprisoned during the final siege of Jerusalem, 32:1-5
    B. Jeremiah bought a field in Anathoth, 32:6-15

        C. Jeremiah's prayer, asking for an explanation, 32:16-25
        D. Yahweh's answer, the people to be restored to the land, 32:26-44
   III. Yahweh's Plans, 33
        A. Making Jerusalem a glory to Himself, 33:1-13
        B. Working through David's Branch, 33:14-26
            1. Executing justice and righteousness, 33:14-16
            2. David's line permanent, 33:17-22
            3. Ruling over the two families, 33:23-26

Significant Themes

1. Beginning Follows End

When the nation hoped against hope that it would be spared, Jeremiah preached doom. When the people were at the point of despair in defeat and exile, Jeremiah preached hope. He proclaimed Yahweh's message of hope through and beyond judgment and exile, not around it.

2. Northern Israel Included

One of the most outstanding features of these oracles of hope is the inclusion of Israel with Judah. References to Jacob, Ephraim, and north country abound in the passage. Scan the chapters for mention of northern Israel. Reunion was part of Jeremiah's vision.

3. Yahweh's Love and Faithfulness

Note 31:9, 20, and 33:11 as examples. What other references to Yahweh's love for His people do you find?

The heart of God is further revealed in the promise, "You shall be my people, and I will be your God" (30:22). Can you find two other places in the Book of Consolation where that promise is made?

Where in the Bible besides Revelation 21:3 does that same goal of God appear? With the help of a concordance note at least three places.

_____   _____   _____

4. Yahweh's New Thing

How God works is pointed out in 31:22. Before jumping to the conclusion that this is a put-down on women, consider what the statement implies. God's means for deliverance and restoration is not force, with a warrior as the hero! The figure implies a reversal of values, and deliverance by a miracle.

5. More Than Return

Restoration usually implies a return to a former state. Israel had made many detours as they rejected God's ways. Jeremiah's hope looks back to the original intent of Yahweh and then forward to fulfillment that goes beyond what had yet been experienced. Return from Babylon to Judah was promised, but the vision was bigger than restoration of political sovereignty and monarchy which were a deviation from Yahweh's will in the first place. The new covenant is a prime example of the moreness of the hope.

The New Covenant (31:31-34)

1. Analysis of the Text

Although not commonly regarded as poetry, this passage has some striking features when the structure is recognized. The RSV text follows, arranged for structural analysis.

"Behold, the days are coming, ... says the Lord,
  when I will make a new covenant
    with the house of Israel
    and the house of Judah,
      not like the covenant
        which I made with their fathers
        when I took them by the hand
        to bring them out of the land of Egypt,
          my covenant which they broke,
            though I was their husband, ... says the Lord.
    But this is the covenant
    which I will make
      with the house of Israel
after those days, ... says the Lord:
    I will put my law within them,
    and I will write it upon their hearts;
    and I will be their God,
    and they shall be my people.
    And no longer shall each man teach his neighbor
        and each . . . his brother,
          saying, 'Know the Lord,'
    for they shall all know me,
        from the least of them
            to the greatest, ... says the Lord;
    for I will forgive their iniquity,
    and I will remember their sin no more."

Look for the repeated words and phrases. Mark them with different colors or in different ways (circles, boxes, straight lines, wavy lines, etc.) so the key words stand out clearly. You will find "I will" seven times, "says the Lord" four times, "covenant" four times, and more.

2. Summary of the New Covenant
    a. Source—Yahweh
    b. Nature—Mutual responsibility
    c. Goal—God and people relationship
    d. Ground—Forgiveness

e. Newness—Inward change

What features of the new covenant are different from those of the old?

Comparison and Relationship of the Several Covenants

In His covenant with Abraham (Genesis 15) Yahweh took full responsibility for the fulfillment of His promise to Abraham and His seed. Yet human trust was present as it always is in God's salvation relationship. The Mosaic covenant (Exodus 19—24) emphasized the responsibility of human response. Based on Yahweh's prior action (Exodus 19:2), the law should not be thought of as a way to earn salvation but as a pattern for response. But God's people abused their freedom and violated and broke the covenant. As a result they suffered exile. But because Yahweh is faithful to His commitment there is return and a new covenant. The Abrahamic, Mosaic, and new covenants come together in Jeremiah.

God fulfills His commitment to be fully responsible for man's salvation. That commitment led to the suffering of the cross. The new covenant rests on God's initiative and love, but it also calls for human commitment and obedience. God writes on the human heart, but it is His law that He writes. "God is at work in [us], both to will and to work for his good pleasure" (Phil. 2:13). It is a covenant of mutual responsibility based on love and freedom.

Careful study requires that we note what the New Testament does and does not pick up out of Jeremiah's predictions. Evaluate these observations:

1. The "new covenant" is seen as established in Jesus Christ.

a. Jesus spoke of the new covenant as being confirmed in His blood (1 Cor. 11:25).

b. Jeremiah 31:31-34 is quoted in full at the beginning of the exposition of the new covenant in Hebrews and summarized at the end (Heb. 8:8-12; 10:16, 17). The New Testament sees the provisions of the new covenant as already being realized in Christ.

2. The New Testament knows nothing of the restoration of Israel as a nation-state in the end times. As David Ewert of the Mennonite Brethren Biblical Seminary, Fresno, California, put it: "But if one accepts the New Testament as God's final revelation, it is hardly legitimate to bypass the New Testament and go straight from the Old Testament to current events, and to affirm that the modern state of Israel is the fulfillment of Old Testament hopes." In the new covenant Jew and Gentile are together in the people of God, without distinction (Rom. 10:12; Eph. 2:11-22). Zion is understood in the New Testament, not as a physical city, but as the church (Heb. 12:22-24).

Participation in the Fulfillment of Jeremiah's Hope

It would be most appropriate to conclude the study of this lesson by celebrating God's love, faithfulness, and miracle with a communion service. Read Hebrews 8:6-12; 9:11-15. Focus on Jeremiah's hope of a new covenant, Jesus' death, Jesus' present reign over the people of God, and the final consummation in Christ in your celebration.

12. Events Before and After the Fall of Jerusalem

Introduction
Focus. The end of the Jeremiah story can be traced through a sizable section of biographical narratives in the latter part of the book. The prophet's life continued to be intertwined with events in Judah. The events before, during, and after the fall of Jerusalem can hardly be related without including Jeremiah the prophet. Of particular interest will be the prophet's role in decisions made during the siege and in the move to Egypt by Jews left behind. Was he honored as a true prophet when his prophecies came true about Nebuchadnezzar bringing death to Jerusalem? We will find some answers in this lesson.

Scripture. Jeremiah 34; 37—44; 52.

Prayer. Yahweh God, Yours is the kingdom and the power. Yet we find You slow to anger and amazingly patient with a rebellious people. We want to know how Jeremiah maintained faith and courage when he was rejected. Be our teacher as we read about the end of Jeremiah's ministry, in the name of Jesus. Amen.

The material in the chapters included in this lesson are largely in the form of biography. Relatively few oracles are mixed in. The material will be treated as a story. Stories are to be read (and told). The approach for this lesson will be a bit different from that employed in previous lessons of this course. Read through the chapters with the help of the outline. A few exercises are included to aid observation and memory. Add your own notes of interest and questions in the space provided.

Events During the Siege of Jerusalem
34:1-7. Message to Zedekiah Concerning the King and the City

Which cities remained unconquered? _____

_____

34:8-22. Freeing and Enslaving of Slaves
Because of disobedience in proclaiming liberty, Yahweh proclaimed liberty of a different kind (v. 17).

37:1-10. Zedekiah's Request for Jeremiah to Pray
   Why did the Chaldeans withdraw from Jerualem? _____
_____

37:11-15. Jeremiah Imprisoned for Alleged Desertion
   Jeremiah's advice in 21:8-10 gives reason to suspect him of deserting.

37:16-21. Zedekiah's Secret Meeting with Jeremiah

   What did Zedekiah ask? _____

   What did Jeremiah ask? _____

_____

38:1-6. Princes Secured Permission to Dispose of Jeremiah

   Why get rid of Jeremiah (v. 4)? _____

_____

38:7-13. Ebed-melech Rescued Jeremiah from the Pit.
   What would you like to say to Ebed-melech? _____

_____

38:14-28. Another Secret Meeting between Zedekiah and Jeremiah

   Why did Zedekiah fear to surrender to the Babylonians? _____

_____

   The weakling that Zedekiah was shows up in these accounts. He wanted Jeremiah to pray for him, perhaps hoping for an optimistic word. Yet he could not walk a straight line in following Yahweh's message to him. He allowed the princes to push him around, yet a slave could rescue Jeremiah. The best he could do was to give Jeremiah a little more protection. The cowardice of Zedekiah stands in sharp contrast to the strength of Jeremiah and Ebed-melech. What is the source of their strength and courage?

The Fall of Jerusalem
39:1-10. The Fall of Jerusalem to the King of Babylon
   What was the last visual memory Zedekiah had in return for running?
_____

39:11-14. Jeremiah Entrusted to Gedaliah
   Who gave command to take care of Jeremiah? _____

39:15-18. Promised Reward for Ebed-melech
    Why did Yahweh promise to spare Ebed-melech? _____

_____

40:1-6. Jeremiah Chose to Stay at Mizpeh
    What is the most surprising element to you in this paragraph?

_____

52:1-23. Jerusalem Captured and Plundered
    Compare this appended chapter (52) with 2 Kings 24:18 ff. for similarities and differences.

52:24-27. Key Persons Executed
    Compare the brutality of the Babylonians with the gentleness observed previously with Jeremiah.

52:28-30. Jewish Captives Taken to Babylon
    Refer to the list of events in Lesson 1 for the dates of the three deportations. What was the total number of captives led away?

_____

52:31-34. Jehoiachin Given Limited Freedom in Babylon
    What value does this paragraph have as the close of the Jeremiah collection?

_____

_____

_____

_____

    Jeremiah had some choices to make. He could go along to Babylon or stay in Judah with the newly appointed governor, Gedaliah. That choice was offered by none other than the high-ranking Chaldean officer, Nebuzaradan. One wonders how Jeremiah felt about being considered a friend of Babylon. The Jewish princes accused him of deserting to the Chaldeans. But his assumed loyalty to Babylon may not have been fully acceptable either. Apparently he could have had an easy time of it in Babylon. He indicated his true loyalty by choosing to stay in Judah. What choice would you have made if you had been in Jeremiah's situation?

Events in Judah after the Fall
40:7-12. Gedaliah Functioned as Governor of Judah
    Gedaliah, appointed by the king of Babylon, appears to be (acceptable, unacceptable) to the remnant in Judah.

40:13—41:10. Ishmael Murdered Gedaliah for the King of Ammon
   What had the years of war done to Ishmael and his associates?

41:11-18. Johanan Rescued the Captives of Ishmael
   Why was there interest in going to Egypt?

42:1-6. The People Sought Yahweh's Guidance through Jeremiah
   What level of credibility did Jeremiah seem to have among the people?

42:7-22. Jeremiah's Answer: "Don't Go to Egypt"
   Is Jeremiah's answer what you expected it to be? How were the people doubly guilty?

43:1-7. Warning Rejected and People Go to Egypt, Taking Jeremiah
   Whom did the people accuse of being the real culprit?

Many strange names are found in the story of Jeremiah. Likely it has gone unnoticed that Gedaliah's family has been part of the story all along. Gedaliah, son of Ahikam, son of Shaphan was part of a much involved family. The family tree is as follows.

```
                        Shaphan (2 Kings 22:3-13)
            _____|_____
            |                |                       |
     Elasah (Jer. 29:3)  Gemariah (Jer. 36:12, 25)  Ahikam (2 Kings 22:11-14)
                             |                       |        (Jer. 26:24)
                         Michaiah (Jer. 36:11)     Gedaliah
```

Turn to the references and find out how various family members have been part of the story. What was their attitude toward Jeremiah?

Events in Egypt with the Remnant
43:8-13. Prediction of Nebuchadnezzar's Conquest of Egypt
   What symbolic act did Jeremiah use to reinforce his message?

44:1-14. Jeremiah Preached Against Worship of Egyptian Gods
   What reason did Jeremiah give for the destruction of Jerusalem?

44:15-19. The People Refused to Give up Worship of the Queen of Heaven.
What reason did the people give for continuing in their idolatry?

44:20-30. Final Prophecy of Punishment for Unfaithfulness
Are these last words from Jeremiah what you would expect to come from his mouth.

What a sad way for the story to end. It's sad with respect to the remnant of Jews in Egypt. They just wouldn't learn. They held to a fundamentally different interpretation of the data of history. It was not obvious to them that Yahweh was speaking through Jeremiah. They were convinced that worship of the gods of the other nations, such as the queen of heaven, was a good thing. They interpreted Josiah's reforms as their downfall.

How must God have felt about such a blind, unteachable people? Bibliodrama is a way of acting out biblical stories in order to get in touch with the feelings and issues. Usually one person takes the role of God, even though he may not speak audibly. Then "God" is asked to share what He saw happening from His perspective. Reflect on the thought of God as He watched the events and attitudes in the closing episodes of the Jeremiah account.

The story is sad with respect to Jeremiah. The people wanted him along, but did not want to listen to him. What must the prophet have felt like when the people defended the practice of idolatry? What must have been going on inside him when the people called his message from Yahweh a lie? As he viewed the whole scope of his ministry in his last days in Egypt, how do you suppose he was feeling about himself and about God? What do you suppose he said to his companion, Baruch, about the turn of events?

One More "Confession"
In an earlier lesson (6) we listened to some of the soul-cries of Jeremiah. As a summary of what you now sense went on in the mind and heart of Jeremiah as he lived through the events just before and after the fall of Jerusalem, write another "confession," as you think Jeremiah might have written it in Egypt. Try to put yourself inside Jeremiah's skin and, in the space below, express your soul communication to Yahweh. What feelings, what doubts, what faith rises to the surface? What do you want to say to Yahweh and what do you hear Him saying to you in response?

13. The Message of Jeremiah, Then and Now

Introduction
Focus. This final lesson in the series will include the steps of review, synthesis, integration, reflection, and worship. We will not be studying any new material from Jeremiah. The lesson is designed to help you consolidate your findings and retain at least some of the learnings from the study of Jeremiah. Consideration will be given to how we get from fifty-two chapters of Jeremiah to life in this part of the twentieth century.

Scripture. Jeremiah 1—52. (We did some "spot picking" in chapters 11—20. If you did not get all the book read at least once, finish any remaining sections as part of this last study.)

Prayer. Yahweh, God of Israel, and Father of our Lord Jesus Christ, You have been speaking to us through the Book of Jeremiah. As we draw these studies to a close, guide our steps of summary and appropriation by Your Spirit. We don't want to miss what You want us to retain and make a part of us. Oversee our study for Jesus' sake. Amen.

Review
1. A Prophet
How would you introduce Jeremiah to someone who does not know him?

_____

_____

What one question would you like to ask Jeremiah about his life?

_____

2. A Book
A friend is reading Jeremiah and asks you, "What about this book of Jeremiah? It is not in chronological order. How is it organized?" How would you respond?

_____

_____

3. *A Section of History*

Is a general outline of the history of the last decades of Judah becoming fixed in your mind?

How much time is covered in the book from the thirteenth year of Josiah to the third deportation in the twenty-third year of Nebuchadnezzar?

_____

What two major events, with dates, are the pivot points for much of the action in Jeremiah?

_____

_____

4. *Themes*

List at least four themes of Jeremiah that seem to be essential elements of his message. (To be refined by study-group discussion.)

_____

_____

_____

_____

_____

_____

Synthesis

Like pieces of a picture puzzle, we have looked at various pieces of Jeremiah's message. Now we need to see what the picture is like when we put the pieces together. For example:

1. What kind of God do we find in Jeremiah? How do the characteristics of the God you find in Jeremiah fit with the God you know? In what ways does the God who reveals Himself in Jesus Christ correspond with the God we find in Jeremiah?

2. What does God want from His people? This is the reverse side, the positive side, of the picture of the charges Yahweh brought against the covenant people. Are expectations and demands the same as in other parts of the Old Testament? How does the picture compare with God's call in the New Testament?

3. What do you conclude about people from the data in the Jeremiah story? What is the composite of human nature as portrayed in Jeremiah? How

much of yourself do you see mirrored in the ways of the Israelites? What is Jeremiah's solution to the problem of perverse human nature?

The synthesis process can and should be applied to many other aspects of a biblical understanding of faith and life.

Integration

Knowledge and understanding are part of the fruit of Bible study, but a head knowledge is not enough. Knowing something does not automatically make that information functional in our lives. Somehow we need to get from the "then" of Jeremiah to the "now" of our lives. Taking bits and pieces out of any part of the Bible and applying them to our lives is not the way God wants us to use His Word. Nor is it a matter of dicovering the principles in Jeremiah and applying those principles to our issues. As William L. Holladay has pointed out in the last chapter of *Jeremiah: Spokesman out of Time*, the purpose of Jeremiah (as of all Scripture) is to lead us into a personal encounter with the same God Jeremiah knew. Obviously it is easier and safer to intellectualize about ideas than to get acquainted with God, but also less rewarding. The various incidents of interaction between God and His people can move us to our own encounter with God, as individuals and above all as communities of faith.

1. What have you integrated into your life out of Jeremiah? What have you been moved to change or strengthen during the course of study?

_____

_____

2. What do you find in Jeremiah that is most meaningful for life today? Build a list in the group session.

_____

_____

_____

_____

_____

Reflection

We need to reflect on a concentrated experience of Bible study such as we have engaged in. Areas for reflection include:

1. What do you appreciate about the Book of Jeremiah now that you did not at the outset of the study?

_____

_____

2. What approaches to Bible study, familiar or new to you, have you found to be especially fruitful? Why?

_____

_____

_____

3. What areas of study in Jeremiah would you like to tag for future work?

_____

_____

Worship
A final element of serious Bible study is worship. God has spoken—through Jeremiah, through His Spirit, and through fellow students and believers. Now what do you want to say to God? Express yourself to God in a written prayer, in verse, or in whatever authentic and creative way you want to respond to God as you now know Him. Prepare your expressions ahead of time and then blend them in a time of praise and worship in the group, not as a show of verbal skills, but as an offering to God.